In Good Times and Bad

Other Books by M. Gary Neuman

Helping Your Kids Cope with Divorce the Sandcastles Way

Emotional Infidelity: How to Affair-Proof Your Marriage and 10 Other Secrets to a Great Relationship

How to Make a Miracle: Finding Incredible Spirituality in Times of Struggle and Happiness

The Truth about Cheating: Why Men Stray and What You Can Do to Prevent It

In Good Times and Bad

Strengthening Your Relationship
When the Going Gets Tough
and the Money Gets Tight

M. GARY NEUMAN
and
MELISA NEUMAN

WILEY

John Wiley & Sons, Inc.

Published by John Wiley & Sons, Inc., Hoboken, New Jersey
Published simultaneously in Canada

For general information about our other products and services, please contact our Customer Care Department within the United States at (800) 762-2974, outside the United States at (317) 572-3993 or fax (317) 572-4002.

Wiley also publishes its books in a variety of electronic formats. Some content that appears in print may not be available in electronic books. For more information about Wiley products, visit our web site at www.wiley.com.

Library of Congress Cataloging-in-Publication Data:

Neuman, M. Gary.
    In good times and bad : strengthening your relationship when the going gets tough and the money gets tight / M. Gary Neuman and Melisa Neuman.
        p. cm.
    Includes index.
    ISBN 978-0-470-53803-6 (cloth)
    1. Marriage—Psychological aspects. 2. Stress (Psychology) 3. Communication. 4. Families. I. Neuman, Melisa, 1966– II. Title.

    HQ734.N484 2010
    646.7'8—dc22

2009031433

Printed in the United States of America

10 9 8 7 6 5 4 3 2 1

For Bonnie
(She knows why)

Contents

CONTENTS

Acknowledgments

Gary: To Oprah Winfrey. Few people truly get the importance of childhood and act on it. I am grateful for your generosity in giving me a platform to help others, especially the children whose lives may have changed as a result of our energy. You improve the quality of life for everyone you touch and inspire others to do their best. It's an honor to work with you to help others. You are an inspiring force of change in our world.

To everyone at Harpo Productions, who put endless effort into the shows I've done. Nobody could imagine all of the work you do to make these programs so wonderful and helpful to others. Thank you, Harriet, Sheri, Lisa. To the go-to person, Katy, I am grateful for your creativity and deep insights into the work that we do. Thanks for your genuine concern for the people we help.

To Dean for always making me so comfortable. Andrea, thanks for commenting, "You know, you could write a whole book on this." Layla, it's a true privilege to work with you. Thanks for being so nice. Gina, your first was the best. Thanks for your graciousness. It's always so great working with you. Rachel, thanks for always listening and for your wonderful energy. Eric, you were great even in freezing temperatures. Thanks, Brad, Gwen, and Kirsten, for your constant help. Joan, thanks so much for the Web site help and for supporting my study. Going back to old times, thanks to Candi, Jim, and Cindy. Thank you all for helping me help others.

Melisa and Gary: To Carol Mann, still doing business on a handshake, thank you for your enthusiasm. We are grateful for the dedication and intelligence you bring to each project. Thank you.

To Tom Miller, thanks for your editorial magic and for taking care of our work, again and again. You are truly dedicated and talented.

To production editor Rachel Meyers, thanks for keeping us all on time. To copy editor Judith Antonelli, thanks for making our work proper.

Our friends and our family gave greatly of their time and insights.

To our parents, thank you for your love, your kindness, your time, and your support.

To Jill, thank you for reading the manuscript, providing excellent suggestions, and always being willing to help.

To Sherri and Jeff, Barbara and Craig, thank you for being there at all times.

ACKNOWLEDGMENTS

To Robin Landers, thank you for your tireless consultations and support throughout this project.

To Dr. Hindie Klein, Reva Kirchblum, Heather and Stephen Kravitz, Malka and Saul Meyerfeld, Lynn Hanau, and Nancy and Marty Engels, thank you for all of your insights, your ideas, and your time.

Thanks to Dr. Donald Hanft, who brings life into the world.

Thanks to Dr. Alfred Jonas, the best of the best.

Many thanks to our children—Yehuda, Esther, Michael, Pacey, and Danny—for being so sweet and interested in the myriad discussions involved in the writing of this book. We love you and are proud of each of you. We are so blessed to have you for our children.

Thanks to the One above Who makes all things possible.

PART ONE

Discover a New Perspective

1

Our Personal Story

None of us wants a difficult struggle in life. We do just about everything we can to avoid it. We want to protect ourselves, our spouses or partners, and our children from any harm. Yet somewhere deep down, we know that our lives bring struggle and that we might develop some character from it. When we review the portions of our lives that have been complicated, we may even come to believe that we've grown through those times and that they have been crucial to our self-growth. Still, we don't want to invite struggle into our lives. We wish away hardship for ourselves and our kids.

There are painful moments in life that do not seem to be worth anything. The pain is so severe that any potential personal development is swamped by the sheer sadness and hurt of the experience.

The bottom line is that we are only partly in control of our lives; we know that it will be necessary to learn to deal with all different types of life experiences. The most important question is the following: How do we come through an experience of difficulty—intact or with a sense of growth? What makes one person, one couple, or one family become stronger through hard times, while others deteriorate and fail?

All of us want to believe that when the going gets tough, our relationships, marriage, and/or family will persevere, grow closer, and develop a renewed meaning of love and togetherness. How utterly disappointing it is when we see our world crumbling around us and begin to feel our family drowning or a relationship becoming more distant. What has happened to us? How do we make it stop? How do we turn it all around?

You can decide right now to make some changes, and within a week you will see your loving relationships change for the better, no matter what your present circumstances. We don't mean to imply that it's easy or that all of your problems will be resolved, but positive change *is* possible. Love is the most powerful, intensely focused tool, and learning to love both yourself and those around you in a healthier way will give you a renewed strength in your life right now.

This book is about change. It will offer you an attitude as well as concrete steps for turning your love life and/or your family life around. You can be one of those people who tells stories about how you not only got through the rough times but also developed a renewed closeness with loved ones through them.

In writing this book, we, Melisa and Gary, chose to reach out to everyone, with examples and stories from people involved in different types of struggles. Although most of our discussion is about financial struggles, we also discuss other serious life events. Coping mechanisms can typically be applied to different stressful situations.

We have always used humor to diffuse our own stress, and this is reflected in our writing style at times. In discussing all these heartfelt matters, we respectfully apply some lightness in an attempt to make difficult issues a little more palatable. We have written with our shared voice, our marital "we," but at times one of us will step out of that voice to share an individual insight that is relevant to the discussion.

Gary recently appeared on *The Oprah Winfrey Show*, where he had the privilege of helping a couple discover how to bring their marriage together after they had separated due to money troubles, job loss, and foreclosure. Afterward he received a letter that criticized him for speaking as if he knew these people's problems. The letter writer assumed that since Gary writes books and was on *Oprah,* he couldn't possibly understand the financial strain that they were under. It was understandable that anyone would be wary of advice from someone who's never been in their shoes.

Therefore, we want to share with you a couple of very personal moments in our marriage, moments that would test anyone's personal and marital strength, with the hope that our sharing will allow you to see where we have been and to understand that the ideas written in this book reflect many of our own life experiences. Everyone's struggles are unique, of course, but we can all learn from one another.

The first personal moment we want to share is our most

significant financial crisis. We were upside down on our mortgage, owing way more than the house was worth, way before this was a common phenomenon—about twenty years ago. We were twenty-one and twenty-three years old, and we had a one-year-old child, a little savings, a baby on the way, and no business buying anything, but as luck would have it, we purchased our first home to be near a new job for which we had moved. It was easy to get a mortgage, and what wasn't covered by our meager savings, we borrowed. The realtor assured us that prices were only going to go up.

Within a year a newer, nicer, rental development was built next door, and real estate prices had tanked. Gary left his job due to internal problems at the company, and nobody was making bids for our home, which we had decided to put on the market. Because of the market and the new competition, our house had lost almost 20 percent of its value. We needed to move quickly to start another job that Gary had gotten, but at less than half his former salary. Many of our purchases for the house and for the new job were being made on our shiny new credit cards.

There we were, with an eighteen-month-old son and a newborn daughter, having to move an hour away but without the means to rent an apartment and still pay the mortgage on the house. We couldn't believe that all our little purchases had grown to such high numbers on the credit cards. We discussed our options with a bankruptcy lawyer, but we wanted to declare bankruptcy only as a last option. We moved into a family-owned condo in South Beach, Florida, near Gary's new job. The condo had belonged to Gary's deceased grandparents and had not been touched for years since their passing. There was no working stove or oven, the cabinet doors hung askew on broken hinges, and the paint was peeling. The pullout couch we slept on had a huge hole in its side. We wondered if an animal had gotten in at some point and chewed the fabric. We both worked during the day and spent nights throwing out furniture and painting, ripping out carpeting, and trying to pay the bills.

We lived in the condo for more than eight months, until we were able to sell our house to the only person who had made an offer on it. We saved and borrowed enough money to pay off the bank and moved into an apartment that actually had a working stove. For the eight months we were in the condo, we cooked in a toaster oven and on one of those burners that you put on top of the counter. We had always wondered who bought those. Now we knew—we did.

Another element of our financial fiasco was that our car was towed, and we realized that the towing fees were worth more than our car was. We ended up signing over the car to the towing company.

The odd thing is that when we remember those months, we talk about them fondly. We remember getting up at five every morning, exhausted, taking our children (who should've been in the *Guinness World Records* book for never, we mean never, sleeping) to feed the seagulls on the beach. Then we would go to the combination coffeehouse and self-service laundry. We really grew, and we made that time into one of the most special moments of our lives. We were grateful for the people who came into our lives and helped us, and we relied on our faith. It wasn't easy, however; we always worried about having enough money for basic expenses. This might have turned into the end of our marriage, but it didn't. In fact, quite the opposite happened. It made us a stronger couple, more in love than ever.

The second personal moment we want to share was on a completely different level of struggle; it concerns our son's illness. Melisa has saved the life of our son, Pacey, on at least two occasions. The first time was when she brought him to the doctor, saying that he seemed lethargic and was crying in the night in an unusual way. She was told that she was being overprotective. We had recently had our fourth and fifth children, twins (one of whom was Pacey) who were now three months old, so we now had five kids under age seven.

In other words, Melisa knew a thing or two about newborns. She led with her intuition and refused to leave Pacey alone. A few hours later she took him to a different doctor, only to be told that if the other doctor had said the baby was fine, she should stop worrying. While in the waiting room, Melisa pointed out that the baby's eyes weren't focused and that he appeared to be having a seizure; the staff there told her that the doctors were at lunch and to go to the emergency room. She decided to leave and race back three blocks to the doctor who had seen them earlier, and by the time she arrived, the baby had lost consciousness. The office staff had lifesaving equipment and stabilized him while the ambulance was dispatched.

It turned out that Pacey had a serious case of bacterial meningitis. After spending four weeks in the hospital, our baby was sent home "healed." We did some exhaustive research and found a world-renowned expert on meningitis, who explained that relapses are very common, and even likely, with this form of meningitis. We had to be highly vigilant about watching Pacey and getting help for him when he needed it.

After one week at home from the hospital, Pacey began to cry in that familiar pained fashion, and we knew that we had a small window of time in which to get him back to the hospital and on intravenous (IV) antibiotics. This would be the second time that Melisa saved his life.

When we rushed back to the hospital on that Saturday morning, we found a twentysomething (our age) pediatrician who met us with raised eyebrows. As she flipped her hair back and chewed some gum, she assured us that Melisa was being an overprotective mother and that our baby looked fine.

Melisa knew the odds: there is an 83 percent mortality rate upon relapse. In other words, Pacey's fever would spike within a very short period. The reason that so many people die from meningitis is that it strikes so quickly. By the time the person reaches a hospital, the body may be way past the point of help.

Melisa demanded that the doctor do a spinal tap on Pacey, because that was the only way to know if the meningitis had returned. The doctor said that the baby could wait, that she first had to make rounds.

Melisa then told the doctor something that has become family lore. She clearly explained that Pacey would most likely be dead after the doctor finished her rounds, and although we didn't have any doctors in our family, we did have many, many lawyers. "You're making a career decision," she curtly told our gum-chewing friend. The doctor made the right choice and did the spinal tap. Within forty-five minutes, Pacey's temperature spiked to 105 degrees, but it was okay because he was already on an IV and the medical staff was taking care of him.

There are many more stories about the year after this. It was a miserable experience that we pray we'll never have to repeat, on any level. Yet we persevered and got through it, and never once did it shake our relationship or our family. That doesn't mean that it didn't shake us up as individuals. Tears flowed down Gary's face on more than one occasion out of sheer stress, and there was a moment that we looked at each other and wondered it we'd ever get out of the hospital with our son. We did, and maybe in part because things turned out okay, we can tell the story today. We can't imagine the alternative, and we marvel at the courage of parents who've had a much different outcome. Their stories, and their insights about how they got through their own difficult times with their relationships intact, will be discussed later in the book.

In this book we bring to you our life experience mixed with our professional experience. Gary has been a family therapist for more than twenty-two years and has written books and completed extensive international research on marital and family issues. Melisa has written for different newspapers and publishes an international column on family and money issues.

Life serves up crazy struggles, and getting through them is a skill that we outline for you in this book. We may make it all sound simple, but we know that it's not. Love is an overwhelmingly powerful force, and we can choose to use it in the best ways possible. We'll show you how to make the right decisions and take the right actions to bring you closer in both good times and bad.

2

The Decision to Fight for Your Relationship

Gary: Recently I traveled to Minnesota on behalf of *The Oprah Winfrey Show* to help counsel Amy and Timothy, a thirtysomething couple with a fifteen-month-old child. Timothy had been making a six-figure salary in the mortgage industry until he was laid off. He hadn't been able to find another job, so Amy and Timothy were losing their house. Timothy had suffered a yearlong depression, and as much as she had tried, Amy was unable to get him out of the basement and away from his Xbox games. Most of the time he wouldn't even get out of bed. He refused help. Understandably, Amy left him. She took the baby and went to live with her mother, who could help her with the baby while Amy was working.

Amy had suffered from melanoma a few years before. Her father had fought melanoma at the same time, but he had passed away. When Amy told me that she didn't have the strength to get through this economic crisis, I brought up her fight with cancer. Clearly, I was looking into the eyes of a courageous, strong woman, and I wanted to help her to see that she could draw on that strength. I asked her how she had the strength to get through cancer, and she responded, "Cancer was easy, compared to this." For me, as a therapist, this was obviously something to explore.

The moment Amy learned that she had cancer, something remarkable happened: she made an immediate decision to live. She was determined to live through it. This belief caused her to do some interesting things. She focused on healing and on bringing into her life anything that would promote her health. Equally important, she refused to listen to anyone who would sap her energy or bombard her with negative statistics.

Amy and I discussed at length that the terms *easy* and *cancer* are not usually spoken together in the same sentence. Surely someone who had stared death in the face and won would find an economic crisis relatively easy, not the opposite. Was it possible that the reason she found beating cancer easier had nothing to do with how much energy she needed for each struggle? That is, it had nothing to do with the *reality* of either situation.

Let's recognize the practical implications of Amy's decision to live. She avoided considerable stress the moment she made the decision. For example, instead of hearing or reading a negative statistic about a woman in her position that would cause her severe distress and require tremendous energy to combat, she skipped right over that process by not listening to or seeing the message in the first place.

Instead of spending hours in turmoil, worrying about her condition, she chose to pretend that the decree for life had been signed, sealed, and delivered. This cut out levels of fear that would have required overwhelming energy to manage.

In bad times, much of our energy is used for combating the inevitable stressful moments, but we lessen the power of those moments every time we decide to fight for our relationship and our family. When you stop entertaining the idea of family disruption, separation, or splitting up, it causes a reduction in worry and stress. It stops conversations about it with others and gives you permission in your own mind to just move forward and focus on the external stressful situation at hand.

When I discussed Amy's marriage with her, her tone was completely different from the way she had talked about her cancer. She admitted that she had never made a decision to fight for her marriage. She had mixed feelings about relationships and trust. Some of her ambivalence was due to her parents' divorce when she was fifteen and the fact that almost everyone in her family was divorced. She almost believed that if she were to divorce, she'd fit in well in her family culture. She told me that even before this economic crisis, she had never fought for her marriage. It simply was not her attitude. Marriage worked as long as Timothy made money and kept that part of the deal.

But when Timothy lost his job and became stuck in his depression, Amy's marriage became very, very hard. Her mother seriously disliked Timothy because he was unemployed. She even convinced Amy that if Timothy didn't make enough money, he should not be allowed to see his child. Amy's mother invited Amy to live with her, and she watched the baby while Amy worked, so Amy's mother was doing a lot to help the situation. But at the same time, her message in support of divorce was so clear that Amy found herself thinking that if she returned to Timothy, she'd be letting her mother and the rest of her family down. Most of Amy's energy was being drained with endless conversations about Timothy and how horrible he was.

Through our counseling, Amy remembered how devastating it was for her to experience her parents' divorce as a teenager. I asked her if she could face her daughter in twenty years and tell her that the reason she had gotten a divorce was that she and Dad had fallen on rough economic times.

At the same time, Timothy was making his own dramatic changes. He got out of his depression, lost forty pounds, spent time visiting with their daughter, and found a place for the family to live (rent-free in exchange for his fixing the place up). He felt horrible for his behavior and apologized profusely for his disconnection from Amy. He'd do anything to save their marriage, but Amy couldn't bring herself to return to it. She didn't know what would happen once she decided to fight for her marriage. How would that change things? How could she renew her marriage just by making the decision to do so?

Sometimes we have to take the plunge, especially when we know it to be a good direction for ourselves and our children. We have to believe that things will work out; then, as a practical matter, our energy can instantly be more efficiently focused on the real problems at hand.

. . .

Amy decided to make her marriage work and to deflect her mother's negative influence. She would be strong and explain to her mother that they would no longer criticize Timothy and that he had equal rights to their daughter in every way. Then an amazing thing happened. Within two weeks, she and Timothy were living together again.

My father-in-law, a circuit court judge for more than thirty years, once told me that the key to relationships is to fight the problems, not each other. Amy began discussing solutions instead of worrying about the problems. It was crucial to her that she never again find herself in the same desperate situation. Timothy agreed that if she ever thought he was depressed, he would seek medical help even if he didn't think he needed it. He put this in writing so that there would be no confusion in the future.

Amy and Timothy began working together as a team, discussing what they could do to resolve their economic issues. I asked them to go on a date, a rather inexpensive one, to allow

Attack the Problem, Not Each Other

Your relationship deserves a fighting spirit. The first and most important step in managing life's struggles as a couple is to decide that you will focus on the struggle as a team, not as two individuals ready to blame each other. Make the decision that your relationship will be strong through these challenges, then listen to nothing else.

themselves permission to reconnect and have fun together. They found renewed energy to tackle their issues together. It would not be an easy task, but when they had each other's help, it instantly became a lot easier. Their economic crisis was still a reality, but the threat of divorce and the ensuing stress were effectively over. Just removing that threat alone freed up major energy for them to deal with the real issue at hand.

What the Fighting Spirit Can Do for You

"While the fighting spirit may not influence your quantity or length of life," says Dr. Steven Greer in an interview for Ben Sherwood's *The Survivors Club: The Secrets and Science That Could Save Your Life,* "it will certainly improve the quality of your remaining time. People with the fighting spirit show far, far less depression, anxiety, and other mental health problems."

If you haven't already done so, make the decision to fight for your marriage, your relationship, and/or your family. Sit with your partner and decide to work together to solve your problems. Write down your commitment on paper. The window of divorce never closes; you can choose that option at any time, but the window for a relationship sometimes stays open for only a limited time. Grab the option while the window is still open and be on your way. Later, we'll outline clearer methods for how to have the conversation with your loved ones, but for now, just recognize the need for the decision. It's the first important answer to getting through and growing through rough times.

Jocelyn's Story: **Why I Decided to Stay with My Husband**

I became a full-time teacher when my youngest child turned ten. My husband, Andre, made a decent living as a hotel manager, and with my income, things were great. We even purchased an apartment near our home that we rented out for extra income. With the recession, however, the hotel business suffered, and the hotel my husband managed suddenly closed. The chain had nowhere else for him to go. I was now the breadwinner, so I had to sign up for summer school teaching. I never wanted to do that. One of the reasons that teaching worked so well for me was that I was always home when my kids were home, so I could be a good mom.

I was angry at Andre for everything. We'd constantly scream at each other. I was mad that he didn't have a better degree, although now I realize that even that would be no guarantee of a better job in this day and age. He tried everything, but the field was cutting back and there was nothing for him. It had been months since we had had sex; usually he'd fall asleep on the couch watching television late at night and just stay there.

It got so bad that our kids begged us during one fight to stop. That's when I realized I'd had enough. I went to my parents and told them I had to separate from Andre. My parents were shocked, because they hadn't known how bad it really was. My father asked me to reconsider and told me to imagine what it must be like for my husband. He explained to me that the stress I was feeling from being the breadwinner was the stress that Andre had felt for eighteen years of the marriage, and suddenly I understood what he was feeling.

I know it must sound crazy, but I was just too consumed with what I was going through to consider how deeply lost my husband was feeling. I'm really not a selfish person; I was simply overwhelmed, and I was used to him taking care of everything. Andre was the fixer. I would always joke with him that he was perfect for the hotel business because he could manage any crisis and make people feel better again. He lost that ability when he lost his job and any hope of getting a new one, and that really rocked me to my core.

Following my father's suggestion, I temporarily turned my thinking around and told Andre how much I was beginning to understand how difficult this was for him. I had never seen my husband tear up before then. He started talking, and for the first time, he let me see the real him. I don't know why, but seeing Andre that way made him so much more real to me. We needed each other in a way that we hadn't before. I told him that it was so hard for me because he was the "fix-it" man, and now I had to be that person. We decided to move back in together and start being a couple again.

The next morning I read in the paper that people were not buying new appliances during the recession;

they were getting their old ones fixed instead. Andre had always been very handy, so I showed him the article and we conceived the idea for him to start fixing things. His grandfather was a plumber, so Andre had grown up understanding how things work.

Within a few months, my husband was making about half the amount of money he had been making at his hotel job. It was helpful that some of the appliances he fixed were brought to us, and we set up the garage as a workplace. My kids have gotten really good at helping their dad, and my fourteen-year-old can now even do some repairs on his own from start to finish.

The kids spend part of their weekends with their dad, helping him with his growing business. I had had one foot out the door, and now we're doing better than we were before all of this mess began. My father is a wise man; he taught me how far a little understanding can go. I'm still teaching summer school, but I believe that spending this time away from my children is still better than divorcing their father would have been. Even if I had gone through with a divorce, I'd still be working in the summer. Now, at least, the kids are home with their dad doing something constructive.

Jocelyn's decision to stay and her husband's positive reaction set the stage for moving out of despair. Once they had decided to work together, she was tuned in to the article in the newspaper, and together they applied it to their lives. If she hadn't been in that frame of mind, it's doubtful that the information in the article would have been applied that way. Her energy would have continued to be too consumed by the negativity and the pain of her situation to allow her to be creative and hopeful. Creativity requires energy, and we have only so much mental and emotional energy to spare. When that energy is exhausted by what's going wrong, we don't have the stamina to figure out how to get things right.

Anthony's Story: It's Not Right to Have Fun at This Time

I was really blessed. I came from a lower-middle-class family and was the first to go to college. My first real estate deal made me more money than my father had made in five years of work as a bricklayer. In the last fifteen years I've done well, and my family has been proud of me. I not only sold many buildings and homes, I purchased other properties and felt secure. Then the real estate office I worked in closed, and some of my properties were put in foreclosure. My father, who was employed part-time, lost his job because construction came to a halt. I never thought so much damage could happen so quickly.

A year ago, when things were still okay, I had gone to a charity auction and bid on a five-day, all-expenses-paid vacation for me and my girlfriend. I had completely forgotten about it and was recently reminded that I had won it and had to use it by a certain date.

My girlfriend really wanted to go, but how could we? For one thing, my ex-wife would then think I was lying when I told her I was suffering financially. Besides, how could I have fun when things were so awful? I was out of work, my father was out of work, the world (it seemed) was out of work, and I was going to go on a tropical island vacation and drink margaritas with my girlfriend?

It was an easy decision. I didn't even want to give the vacation to anyone else. I just let it lapse, and my girlfriend couldn't believe it. She doesn't understand that just because it was paid for doesn't mean that it would have been right to go.

Anthony's thinking is common. Basically, when things are tough, we're supposed to be sad and forlorn. We're supposed to be fighting our way through, just barely staying above depression, and we're certainly not supposed to be laughing and having fun.

Anthony is wrong, however.

His point is understandable, but he is simply building misery for himself. All of us need, at some point, to regain our composure, reclaim life, and move on. This may be after a day, a month, or a year or more of sadness and pain. The human mind has to allow itself not to sink so low that it can no longer function properly. If a person loses balance and the ability to properly function, then medication or other external help may be indicated. In most situations, however, the mind and the body themselves will dig themselves out of the slump they are in, and get back to living in the way you once knew. Letting go of anger or moving through a bad time is something that people do on their own schedules.

Let's give ourselves permission to live again. How we do this will be different for every person, but when it happens it is unmistakable. We grant ourselves the right to stop suffering the way we have been suffering. We simply get tired of being angry or unhappy. Feelings are feelings; one passes, then another one comes along. Who's to say how long you "have to be" angry or unhappy? Who's to say how anyone "should" feel in a given situation?

Change Your Place for a Fresh Viewpoint

You might find a different perspective or a new side of yourself if you get away from your normal surroundings. This is especially true of people who vacation in places that are sentimental to them, like childhood vacation spots. We have been to some of the most expensive hotels in the world, yet the small inexpensive beach motel where our family has gathered for forty years remains the place we love to visit when we're down or when we want to celebrate something.

Some people don't realize how helpful it can be to take the time to go away together. One couple found a cruise package that cost them thirty-five dollars a day per person, including all food and entertainment. Other people swap houses through a Web site; they find that a change of pace helps them to reevaluate things in many ways.

The more negativity we focus on, the more stuck and hopeless we become. The more we encourage hopefulness and are positive that we'll get through this financial crunch, the more likely it will be to happen. Some would say it's because of the universe's propensity to match your energy. Maybe that's true. But it's your determination that helps you find creative energy and a renewed sense of hopefulness.

Make the Choice to Be Lucky

In *The Luck Factor: The Four Essential Principles*, Dr. Richard Wiseman writes that lucky people maximize chance opportunities. To conduct an experiment, he had different people, those who considered themselves lucky and those who viewed themselves as unlucky, meet him in a coffeeshop for an interview. Wiseman placed a five-dollar bill on the step leading up to the coffee shop. The "lucky" people saw the bill, picked it up, and told others what a great and lucky day it was. The self-described "unlucky" people didn't even notice the five-dollar bill.

There have been many studies on the remarkable effects of optimism on our lives. One study followed thousands of Minnesotans who took a personality test in the 1960s. Those who scored highest on pessimism were about 30 percent more likely to exhibit signs of dementia up to four decades later. Another study found that pessimistic college students experienced more psychological and physical problems than optimistic college students did. The optimistic students experienced less stress and depression and were more likely to seek social support.

Studies repeatedly show that a positive attitude has very practical implications. Imagine that you will heal better physically with a positive attitude and a loving spouse next to your hospital bed. It's not magic. Your attitude will cause different thoughts, stresses, and concerns. What your mind and your body will have to deal with will change, causing you to have a different vision. Add your spirit and the metaphysical considerations to the mix, and there's no end to what your attitude and your mood can do to help you through life's struggles.

You have a choice. You can wait indefinitely for your mind, your body, and your soul to allow yourself to exercise a positive attitude and enjoy life, or you can decide to consciously do it right now. Why wait? Whom are you pleasing? Whose rules are you following? Who has the right to say how long you "should" be unhappy or not enjoy life to its fullest? Do you have to wait for financial good times to return in order to have good times, or can you find some good in life just because you've decided to make it so? Give yourself permission to feel the positive or good feelings that come your way even when times are tough.

When we were in the hospital with our newborn son, Pacey, we never left him alone. Since we had an identical newborn twin at home as well, this meant that one of us had to sleep in the hospital room while one of us stayed home. We switched off and made it work to the best of our ability. In the third week, Gary's mom came to town, and being the wonderful mother that she was, she stayed with us for a few nights and helped with the kids.

At this point Pacey was safe, and we simply had to give him antibiotics long enough to feel secure that the infection wouldn't return. One night we decided to go out and try to enjoy ourselves. It had been too long since we had been together in this way. We could've found many reasons not to do it. Both of our mothers were helping out, one in the hospital and one with our other children, but was it appropriate for us to go out and have fun? What might people from town think, knowing that we had a sick child and seeing us out laughing and having fun?

When we were living in South Beach, taking jitneys to save a quarter a day, we still made the effort to have fun. We rented bikes with baby seats for three dollars an hour and enjoyed ourselves. We could have

Give to Others

One good way to feel positive in trying times is to give to others. Practicing acts of kindness in your family and in the world lifts your mood and benefits others. Give in all ways, large and small, and focus on the positive feelings you create in others.

just lived in stress and been angry at each other because of the uncomfortable situation we were in. We could have decided to wait until we had more money, when we could afford nice restaurant dinners, and *then* have fun. But why wait? Why does having or not having a lot of money dictate whether we enjoy our lives? Obviously, there are things a family can and cannot do to have fun due to the cost, but being allowed to enjoy life is not based on money. It's your personal choice.

Many couples stop having sex, stop going out on dates, and just stop laughing when a bad time strikes. What they forget is that living life to its fullest can't wait for some time in the future. It may be diminished by present circumstances, but there aren't different parts of life, the good and the bad. It's all life, and it's all what we choose to do with it.

When are we more likely to creatively address our issues:

Give Yourself Permission to Be Happy

Consider what could be holding you back from giving yourself permission to enjoy life. Do you believe that you're not entitled to have positive feelings? Are there people who would be uncomfortable with your being happy now? Challenge yourself to make the decision that you are allowed to feel good, to engage in and create better times in your life right now.

If I were more hopeful and happy right now:

1. What would my parents think?
2. What would my spouse or partner think?
3. What would my friends think?
4. What would my children think?

Answer these questions so that you can be clear on any stumbling blocks that prevent you from allowing yourself to enjoy this moment. You will, we hope, see the importance of how your loved ones (especially your children, if you have them) would benefit from your positive attitude during this time and how you can determine to turn things around. Forget about what the world may think. You do not have to cooperate with social expectations to feel unhappy because of your present situation.

when we're feeling obligated to be unhappy and overwhelmed, or when we're allowing ourselves to be in love and trying our best to be hopeful? The experience of shutting out the good moments in life causes more sad moments and discourages the creative, hopeful energy that enables us to make better choices to change our circumstances.

Anthony was doing himself no favor wasting the trip for some idea of what he "should" be doing. If he truly didn't want to go, he could have offered the trip to someone else or tried to sell it. He could have gone on the trip, networked with people, used the time to get a little more sleep, and have had an idea or an experience that could help him move toward a stronger financial future. Most good ideas and connections in life don't come from a specific plan. The more we allow ourselves to be open to different experiences, the more chances we have to find solutions.

Alfred Nobel: Finding a Constructive Side in the Destructive

Alfred Nobel was an extraordinarily wealthy man. Few know that he acquired his fortune by developing dynamite. His intention might have been to use it as a tool for construction, but it was quickly used in wartime to destroy and kill.

Toward the end of his life, Nobel read something that shocked him. An erroneous publication in 1888 of a premature obituary of Nobel by a French newspaper condemned him for his invention of dynamite. The obituary stated, "The merchant of death is dead," and went on to say, "Dr. Alfred Nobel, who became rich by finding ways to kill more people faster than ever before, died yesterday."

At this point, Nobel could understandably have become quite upset. He might have spent months lamenting his life's work, his legacy of death. Apparently, however, his spirit would have none of that. He decided to do something wonderful for the world and put money into a fund that would award prizes to those who promote peace in the world—the antidote to his dynamite killing force. On November 27, 1895, at the Swedish-Norwegian Club in Paris, Nobel signed his last will and testament and set aside the bulk of his estate to establish the Nobel prizes, to be awarded annually without distinction of nationality. He left an amount that today, allowing for inflation, would be hundreds of millions of dollars. When we think of this man, we have only one image of him: the founder of the Nobel prizes. At a moment of sadness and potential despair he was determined not to give up but instead to do something to change his legacy and give hope to the world. The Nobel Peace Prize in particular continues to focus us all on hope even today, more than a century after he started it.

Just as Nobel did in 1895, we can take action to make ourselves feel better about a given situation. There are indeed many difficult circumstances in which it's almost impossible not to be disappointed, no matter how much positive thinking we do. Forcing "happiness" by denying reality isn't healthy, either; sometimes we need to feel sad, or else we'd be denying genuine feelings. But we can still find moments of hope, calm, and love even during sadness. We can still work to be close to our loved ones in any period, in good times and bad.

3

The Moment to Save (or Lose) Your Relationship

In difficult times, many couples, usually without ever noticing it, start dealing with life as individuals. They begin to recede from each other and allow a distance to develop. They stop talking. They find their feelings to be too intense and too difficult to face, so they don't share them. They don't want to share that they are scared, so each partner says nothing and goes into a deep and lonely place within. They don't fight for their relationship. Instead they fight over money and who's at fault in the situation. They blame each other for not making enough money, for spending too much money, for not saving money, or for not spending enough time doing the things that will bring in more money.

≈≈≈≈≈≈≈≈≈≈≈≈≈≈≈≈≈≈≈≈≈

What's Your Moment?

In order to become a whole couple again, you probably need to realize that you made a decision to pass by your healing moment and thus allowed the distance to grow. At times it may seem easier not to talk, to instead just walk away or go to sleep and never discuss the issues. Who wants to deal with anything uncomfortable, if you don't have to? Make no mistake, however: when you walk away, you are making a decision to leave the part-nership and go it alone. That one time leads to the next, and before long a pattern of creating distance is set. It happens quickly, because you go from not dealing with it tonight to wondering, months or years later, how the two of you got so far apart.

Make your moment the time to decide that you will fight for your relationship. Come together and spend time sharing, talking, and just being together. As soon as you

≈≈≈≈≈≈≈≈≈≈≈≈≈≈≈≈≈≈≈≈≈

Gary can't remember hearing how one of these fights actually encouraged someone to make or save more money. He doesn't recall anyone ever telling him, "I wasn't working hard enough, until one night my partner let me have it and screamed and yelled and humiliated me. I felt like a complete and utter failure, and, boy, did that get my work ethic to kick right in."

When a couple grows apart, their passion recedes. Very

see yourself or your partner receding, do something about it. Plan time to go out together, say how much you love and care for each other, and give each other simple reassurances, such as "we'll get through this together, we can depend on each other, and we have to make it work for us and our family."

If you are like most people in a relationship, you can look back and notice that somewhere along the line, you lost the moment when you could fight for your relationship and attack the problems in life together instead of attacking each other. You can resolve any distance you have, but it starts with a new moment in which you decide to create a new, or truer, combined lens through which to view life together. It starts with the moment you decide to diligently work to come together and make your relationship and the love within it the primary focus of your life.

quickly, two apparent strangers are sharing a life. Once the decision to step back from each other has been made, the rate of distancing speeds up. It becomes harder to make the decision to come together and regain the rhythm of a partnership that allows you to share, seeing life through one lens.

From that moment, it is a short step from living together to merely residing together. The partners begin to take very separate paths and have little intimacy. They fall into a pattern of individual distance and may still have some limited good times here and there, but so much of their lives remains unshared. They might share their experiences with each other from time to time, but the decision to work toward a singular combined life attitude has become lost to them. They soon find themselves rarely having sex, going out only with other couples, and generally seeing alone time together as the exception to the rule. They wake up from this lifestyle when the distance becomes so wide that they finally realize that they are not a true couple; then, unfortunately, they are at the point of not even knowing where to begin to change the situation. They are at a loss for how to become a unit again.

Now Is the Time to Start Anew

Life offers us so many diversions that once we emotionally leave our relationship, we can fill our void with work, friends, children, and play without missing a beat. Soon any spare moment is used up with something other than our partner. The only time we spend together is the time we have to, and we try to keep it short and do something that doesn't require much conversation (movie, anyone?). You lose your groove fast. This is why it's crucial to turn away from that moment of distance and force yourselves to make a moment of determination to be close.

When you make the decision to get through any struggle together, it builds on itself in a positive direction with the same intensity. Just that one time you don't walk away—when you talk through the issues, share your complicated feelings, and tell each other how much you need each other instead of going it alone—instantly sets a clear precedent that makes it easier and easier to come together every day thereafter.

Soon it becomes natural to spend time together and seek each other out regularly. You sleep together, make love, have some relaxed time, and allow the other to be of help and support. Remember how far a little love goes. A lover doesn't always have a clear answer, but a simple hug, kiss, compliment, or sincere and sympathetic tear will do wonders for the soul. Use your partner to feel heard and understood. Use the moment to decide firmly that no matter what, nothing will get in your way of a loving relationship. It's your partnership, and the two of you are in complete control of it. Nothing on the outside can hurt it.

Carmela's Story: **The Life-Changing Letter**

I was burning mad at my husband, Jorge, and we hadn't slept together in weeks. He was ungrateful, and I just couldn't imagine how we were going to remain together. My father had given Jorge a job in the family furniture manufacturing company. It worked okay for the past few years, but I was forced to be the go-between. My father would tell me what Jorge could do better, and it became my place to relay the information. My father explained that he had only given Jorge a job to help me out, so it would be my job to manage him.

One day, Jorge was fired. He was caught in a meeting with one of my father's rivals, talking about going to work for him. He had brought the rival all sorts of designs and insider information from my father's business. Forget the economic disaster he caused by throwing away a perfectly good job. Now I had to deal with my father and his ranting about what Jorge had done. What a mess Jorge had put me in.

Jorge came home angry at my father and even angrier at me because I was already aware of the news. He exploded, and I gave it right back to him. We shouted, then he stormed out of the house. When he returned, we were only too happy to avoid each other. He played with the kids a bit and fell asleep on the couch.

The next weeks were full of tense and meaningless chatter. Our busy lives carried on as we took care of the kids and managed the house. He sought other job opportunities and practically moved into the kids' playroom, which doubled as a guest room.

One afternoon a month later I received an e-mail from Jorge. It read: "Carmela, this stinks. I've had some time to think about it and if you want me to leave, I'll go, but I want to talk about the kids and how much I can see them before I leave. I'm not going to be one of those visiting dads. But you should know that the meeting I had was not at all what you or your father thinks. Basically, I'd heard that our competitor was thinking about selling, and I thought it would be great if I could lead the way in finding out about it and bringing it to your father. But when your father somehow found out and fired me, didn't even talk to me about it, I said the hell with it. I'm not kissing up anymore. I know I haven't been the best provider, and maybe you shouldn't trust me, but this is the truth, and you didn't give me a chance to explain. I wasn't going to tell you, but before I left I thought you should know. For the kids' sake if not for our own. Yes, I still love you. Let me know what you want to do."

I replied with an apology and agreed to talk about it. This time we both really listened to each other, and it became pretty simple to show each other our love. We slept together for the first time in a month.

Things Can Change in an Instant

Isn't it amazing how things can go wrong so quickly and then go right again? Carmela and Jorge were considering divorce, but after one conversation they were back on track. It sounds like a story made up in Hollywood, but it's the truth. Sometimes we still have the same love for each other, but we make the decision to cover it up and focus on the problems and the hurt. That negative focus in turn causes us to scream and push each other away. The toxicity builds quickly, and if a couple does not avoid it, it just settles in.

When either person decides to do something positive about the situation, it sends a completely different message: let's focus on us, the love we've shared, the kids we've brought into this world, and how we can get through this together. The honest sharing of thoughts and feelings, no matter how complicated, brings us into the inner sanctum of our psyches. That in itself sends a message of togetherness.

Just turning to your partner with the desire to share says, "I love you, and I want to depend on you." That powerful message moves a couple away from fighting and into caring and problem solving. We feel simultaneously stronger and more peaceful when we know that someone who loves us is in our corner and is working through this with us. This knowledge builds on itself. In some cases, like the case of Carmela and Jorge, it can even turn people on the brink of marital disaster back to a loving focus on each other and their family.

PART TWO

Transform Your Relationship

4

What Money Really Means to You and Your Partner

Money represents many different things to different people. Money issues are often not about finances at all. Whenever people are arguing about money, Gary, as a therapist, looks for the underlying issue.

When Justin and Marilyn argued about money, it was World War III. Crazy, huh? Money bringing people to such hostility? That's because the argument wasn't really about money at all. He had lost his job, and she was supporting the family now. Justin had been in total charge of the money and believed that it was his, primarily, because he earned it, while Marilyn had a part-time job just to keep her active in her field of law. Now the pendulum had swung, and she was working more than ever.

They were living off her salary and their rapidly dwindling savings.

Their money fights were illogical. Justin and Marilyn should have been sitting and carefully plotting their next move, brainstorming creative ways for Justin to get back into the job market and coming up with serious strategies to manage their spending. Getting out and talking to others about how they were coping would have been productive. Fighting bitterly about who was at fault and how each one let the other one down was a waste of time.

The money was merely a representation of something far more important. Marilyn lost respect for Justin because she thought that he couldn't take care of her anymore and wasn't prepared for the recession. She admitted that he really hadn't done anything wrong but that his cavalier attitude made her angry.

Marilyn wanted to be taken care of and feel the way she had felt when Justin had earned the money and paid the bills; that had been his way of caring for her. When that came to a screeching halt, she felt threatened. Justin thought that Marilyn had no sympathy for his situation and had not curtailed her spending when the economic situation started to look bad.

Anyone could have told him that it wasn't Marilyn's spending in the two months before he lost his job that put them in this hole. Still, he felt abused by her because she expected him to just make money, no matter what. He interpreted his wife's behavior as aggressive and was angry about it. He expressed no appreciation for her taking on the burden of full-time work and didn't see why he should feel remorse. Justin couldn't imagine that his actions and lack of expression made Marilyn feel uncared for.

They were stuck talking about money when the deeper issue was really that neither partner felt cared for by the other. That was something they both had to explore. They needed to figure out how to care for each other and have sympathy for each other in many ways, not just financial ones. Once they could recognize the root of the problem, they could express their feelings, listen, and care for each other, without letting their preconceived notions from childhood and society about the meaning of money get in the way of their friendship and their love for each other.

Complete this exercise to better understand your relationship with money. What follows is a list of the many things that money can offer us. Circle the ones with which you identify. Then put a check next to the ones that really speak to you.

Money gives me a sense of:

Control

Power and strength

Diversion from my other issues

Being able to care for others

Being cared for

Being able to maintain my health

Fun

Being able to rest and take it easy

Personal acceptance

Social acceptance

Value

Importance

Feeling better than others

Feeling attractive and beautiful

Accomplishment

Success

Safety

Calm and peace

Being right and recognized as knowledgeable

Trust

Now answer this question:

If I had more money than I knew what to do with, how would my life change?

Your responses in this exercise will tell you a lot about what you think money offers you. Recognizing the different things that money means to you will help you to get through tough financial times. If money gives you a sense of control, then maybe you can realize that control is an illusion. Having more or less money may dictate how you spend your day, but that's about it. Money is not magic dust that protects you from harm, pain, divorce, or acid reflux.

Do you want a close relationship with your spouse and kids? You don't need money for that. It's true that you might have less time with them because you have to work a second job, but you can creatively have close, meaningful times with your family when you are together. Do you want a pretty home? Make it happen. You don't have to spend money on a decorator who will

20/20 Foresight

We love to say that hindsight is 20/20; if only we had known then what we know now. Let's have some foresight so we can avoid this message to ourselves. Imagine yourself one year from today. What would you like to be saying to yourself, your mate, your children, and your friends? Wouldn't it be wonderful if you said something like "Sure, it was tough going, but I really got to spend some more time with my kids, my friends, and my partner, and I feel closer to them. I was able to become more involved in giving, and we all really learned what family is all about."

give you ideas that you can find in magazines. Find an item that you love, buy that one, and wait for the rest. You don't have to feel shortchanged if you focus on your goal and use creativity to get there. Even when you did have more money, you certainly had your share of limitations.

Life can't wait for money, and it really doesn't have to do so. Kindness, love, caring warmth, fun, and family togetherness never were and never will be the sole privilege of the well-to-do. Deal with the situation you have and create from it something of which you'll be proud. Find alternate ways of getting the feelings you get from money so that money doesn't decide for you how you're going to feel. Take control over your own life and find ways to experience the feelings that are important to you.

.   .   .

Justin and Marilyn were on a crash course with a huge disconnect between them. They were becoming angrier and angrier and not dealing with the deeper issues at hand. Once they were able to pick out words in the money and feelings exercise, they could discuss ways to get from each other what they couldn't get from money.

Justin honed in on accomplishment, and Marilyn focused on being cared for. They articulated what they needed and talked about how to help each other meet those needs. Marilyn had no idea that her husband's sense of accomplishment in life was being compromised. She saw him as such a success from the past that to her it seemed ridiculous that he'd judge himself differently because a worldwide economic issue had diminished his present earning power. Justin was equally surprised that his spending on his wife gave her a sense of being cared for, and he felt bad that he could no longer provide that. He realized that because he wasn't a touchy-feely kind of guy, his wife resorted to his financial giving as a substitute for other, more emotional displays of caring.

They were able to discuss the deeper issues as well as smart, loving solutions for their emotional needs. Marilyn reminded Justin what an accomplished person he still was. She had never realized how important it was for him to hear compliments. He had seemed so hardened and confident, but now she saw him in a different light and was happy to offer him more sincere positive feedback in the future. Justin knew that he had to offer other ways of making his wife feel cared for: giving more help at home, showing more affection, and taking the time to listen to and appreciate her new challenges on the job. It wasn't difficult or time-consuming, but he had just not been the type of person to focus on that, so he was willing to work on that part of himself. He admitted that he wanted to be more expressive with his kids as well. Now was the best time to begin.

Suddenly, a couple who had been entangled in an angry crisis turned things around by finding the deeper meaning of their money and looking at new solutions for reaching their goal: not money itself, but the feelings that money once gave them.

Hank and Cindy's Story: The Delayed Wedding

Hank was what they call a man's man. Tall, well built, and suntanned, he was a good fit for his career. He worked for a boat company and had climbed his way up the corporate ladder; he now represented the company for the entire southeast region of the United States. When economic woes hit the country, sales on luxury items like boats tumbled, and Hank was reduced to a holding pattern. He still had a job, but since the real money that came his way was in bonuses and commissions, he was looking at approximately an 80 percent reduction in income in one year.

Hank had lived with Cindy for three years, and they planned to get married. When the money flow diminished, Hank went into an emotional tailspin and told Cindy that the wedding would have to wait until he had enough money again. All his savings were going to be used to pay for expenses until the economic situation improved.

Cindy was deeply hurt. She saw herself invested in a four-year relationship with a man who had cold feet. How much money he made didn't influence her decision to marry, and she wondered why it made such a difference to Hank. Cindy worked as a nurse, and although her income was well below what Hank was used to making, her salary was legitimate and enough to cover basic expenses. She was disheartened and felt completely disregarded as Hank became increasingly clear about his decision, and this led to their temporarily breaking up.

Cindy agreed to do the money and feelings exercise with Gary. She reviewed the list, and Hank agreed to do the same. They discovered many crucial things about themselves and their relationship to money. Hank chose many items from the list: power and strength, fun, social acceptance, value, importance, success, and being right. Hank was now able to articulate to Cindy that his job afforded him much more than dollars.

Hank had never finished high school. Being a big-time boat salesman brought him into a society that was impossible for him to reach otherwise—or so he believed. He rubbed elbows with the wealthy and famous and felt included in an elite group. The job was a full package of identity for him; without it he thought of himself as just a high school dropout. His wife-to-be had a nursing degree and was accomplished in the fields of education and science. Compared to her, he felt poor, stupid, and valueless.

He feared that he would begin to resent her ability to make money and support them and that she would be seen as the smarter of the two. He'd feel completely unaccomplished around her. He didn't want to let her go, but felt stuck, as if he had no choice but to get himself back to where he had been. He could think of nothing else.

This discovery was huge for Cindy. She had felt angry as a result of assuming that after several years, he had simply decided that he wasn't attracted to her or that she wasn't good enough for him. The fact that it was quite the other way around was astonishing to her. From the list in the money and feelings exercise, she chose the ability to care for others, fun, and feeling attractive and beautiful. Over their years together, their money had given Hank and Cindy entry to a group of people who supported various charities, and they had attended many charity dinners. Cindy took tremendous pride in giving from her own earnings, since her living expenses were taken care of by Hank. That would now change. There would be little or no money for donations, surely not on the level of giving she'd become accustomed to.

They had been way off in what they believed about each other's connections to money. Clearing the air gave them new hope in their relationship. They had to discuss ways of getting past these issues and how each of them could help shore up the other's sense of weakness.

Hank had to stop the high school dropout references

and comparisons to Cindy. Just hearing him say it gave her the chance to explain that she didn't think of him that way, and he seemed to believe her. The moment they reassured each other, they were able to relax.

Soon they started to discuss solutions. He could surely get his general equivalency diploma and start taking some online college courses. As long as she didn't see him as stupid compared to herself, he felt much calmer. Cindy's belief in Hank allowed him to believe in himself. Cindy's concerns over her looks were alleviated when Hank told her that he sincerely found her beautiful and sexy. They'd been angry at each other for so long that this kind of talk had become impossible for them.

They decided to practice giving by feeding the homeless and visiting the local hospital's children's cancer ward. Before Hank lost his job, they had been discussing starting a family, and they had known then that when they did, their lifestyle would have to change, regardless of how Hank's job developed.

They came to realize that there is a time and a place for everything and that instead of lamenting the end of one stage of their lives, they could celebrate having experienced it. No longer did they view the fun, high-style life as being ripped away from them; instead they decided they were trading it in for a quieter, family lifestyle. Hank would look for sales jobs in other areas that would keep him closer to home. Discovering the meaning beneath their money brought them back to the table to discuss the real issues and stop fighting about money.

Fear of Money

One of the most complicated issues about money is how much we fear it. You may not think of it in that way, but there is a level of fear in most people about making money, creating more income, saving it, and knowing whom to trust with it.

A woman who lost her fortune to Bernie Madoff explained to Gary why she had given every last dime to Madoff to manage for her: she had been afraid. She didn't know what to do with her money, and she was worried that she would do the wrong thing or make the wrong investments. She didn't understand how the financial markets worked, and she was nervous about financial investment, so she trusted someone else to take care of it all. Some of us are better at making money than knowing what to do with it once we have it.

This woman's thinking isn't much different from the thinking of a sick person who chooses to give away control over his decisions. The more fear he experiences, the more he wants to surrender to the doctor to do whatever she thinks is best. Fear causes us to succumb and remain ignorant about issues we really need to understand. When we are afraid of something, we'd rather not look at the issue; we'd rather let someone else make decisions for us, even though we know they might not be the right ones.

Norma and Al's Story: Ignoring the Facts and Hoping They'll Go Away

Norma and Al lost much of their stock investment. It represented a great deal of their collectively hard-earned money. They argued about what to do, and they agreed that they should sell their stock at a loss because it was probably just going to dip further. Still, neither of them did anything. It became so bad that when the monthly account statements came in, they just threw them out without opening them.

Norma explained embarrassedly, "It was just so painful to see our money dwindle. You just get to the point where you don't want to look at it. Instead you keep hoping it'll all be over and you'll be told that everything is back where it was. Then we'd fight over why the other one didn't follow through. I, of course, played the man card. You're the guy, you do this, blah blah blah. That drove him crazy, probably because he did feel like a fool as a man who didn't sell our stock when we knew it was dropping. He'd throw it in my face that I could've sold it. I don't support him in anything. He's working like a dog to make a living and can't deal with this stress. I played dumb, like I couldn't figure out how to call the account manager and make it happen. I just couldn't deal with it. It was like we'd rather ignore it and have it all go away so we could make believe it never happened. Dealing with it represented a real loss."

Unfortunately, Norma and Al's stock portfolio

dwindled to 21 percent of its original value. "Had we sold it even when it lost 50 percent and just put it in the bank or paid off our mortgage, we'd be feeling a whole lot better," Norma said. They would have a lot more money, too, as well as the experience of working together as a team instead of falling victim to all of the prolonged anger and blame in their marriage.

Rosa's Story: The Cost of Fear

Rosa had worked at a government job for twenty-three years. There were rumors, then meetings about budget cuts and people losing their jobs. Rosa was truly paralyzed over the possibility of being out of work and having to find a new job after being in the same one for so many years. This fear stopped her from opening e-mails from work about retirement programs, knowing that she had years to go.

She lost her job within two months and walked away heartbroken. She found out later that if she'd only reviewed the e-mails and letters, she'd have noticed that she was eligible for a retirement package. It wasn't as good as what she would have gotten at regular retirement age, but it was a retirement package nonetheless. She felt like an idiot but remembered how overwhelmed with life she was. Her daughter, a single mother of two, was living with Rosa so that she could help them out financially and emotionally. She just couldn't deal with another stress.

A friend told her to contact an attorney to see if she could do anything about the retirement package after the fact, but Rosa claimed to be too tired and said that she'd feel foolish just having to tell the story.

It can be hard for some people to believe how much fear can paralyze us. This past year, a dear friend of ours passed away from colon cancer. She had lived with certain fears, and one of them was a fear of doctors. She was a warm, giving individual, and we spent several hours with her each week during her final months. She told us that she had ignored symptoms—first pain, then bleeding—until she summoned up the courage to go to a doctor. Early detection of colon cancer can dramatically

When You're Afraid and Would Rather Not Deal with It

If you find yourself becoming paralyzed by fear, ask your spouse to help you out. Your partner won't have the same emotional attachment as you, so he or she will be able to look objectively at the situation with you. Be direct. Force yourself to tell your partner to push you, so that together you can take action when you don't want to, whether it's going to the doctor, the dentist, an attorney, a bank, or an employer.

improve the chance of survival. She knew that had she sought out a doctor at the first sign of symptoms or had a routine colonoscopy, the likelihood of her living would have tremendously increased.

We write this with sadness, not only because we lost our friend but because she suffered. In the end she was forced to overcome her fear anyway, in a big way, in order to endure the painful treatments. Allowing our fears to paralyze us usually leads to very unpleasant situations, in which we are forced to overcome the same fears we had been avoiding in the first place. Forcing ourselves into the uncomfortable place of looking at what we'd prefer to avoid can save our lives, our homes, and our relationships.

Melisa's father, a circuit court judge, told us how unfortunate it is when people's homes are in foreclosure and they don't show up for the hearings. He explained that when people come and tell their story, he can try to help them and grant them more time. If they don't show up, however, there's nothing he can do. People are so worried that they are afraid to even show up in court without an attorney and just talk to the judge, when that is the very thing that could save their houses for them.

It's crucial to lose this fear. The worst-case scenario can be harsh, but you can still have your loved ones, warmth and kindness, and spirituality—all the really important things in life—with or without your money. You can counter a bad situation, financial or otherwise, with clear thinking, the support of loved ones, and creative energy. If you seem to be losing ground, ask your spouse, your partner, or even a good friend to help you. Even people who are not good at helping themselves can be helpful to you; the fact that it's not their money, their job, or their home can actually free up their energy to think straight and creatively. They won't attach the fear and anxiety to it that may be paralyzing you.

Do something. Don't be afraid to look your situation straight in the eye and take any action that might help.

5

What You Learned about Money

We learn about money quite early from our parents. Attitudes about what money means to you, who works for it, to whom it belongs, and what its true purpose is are formed in you in childhood, and you are drawing on those lessons today, whether or not you realize it.

Jerry's Story: Rejecting Dad's Influence

It was like clockwork: every Saturday morning my father would sit at the little desk in his bedroom and pick up a pile of envelopes. The checkbook would come out, and my two sisters and my brother knew to run like the wind. Within ten minutes, we'd hear Dad yell my mother's name repeatedly: "Alice, Alice." She would never respond to the first two calls, but somewhere between the third and the fourth, she'd run upstairs as if she had no idea what was going to happen.

A fight would begin. It was always about how much our mother spent, that she couldn't account for certain checks, and that she was making things impossible for my father. I had different opinions about this at various stages in my life. I always disliked my father's attacking behavior, but there was a time that I felt bad for the old boy having a wife who was spending him into poverty by buying all that stuff.

I remember being eight years old and telling my mother not to buy stuff, because she was obviously the reason we didn't have enough money. I also thought that maybe if I did this, Dad wouldn't scream at her on Saturday. I always felt guilty because Mom couldn't stop spending, and often her spending was on me and my siblings. She'd buy us ice cream at the department store and a pack of baseball cards with a free stick of gum inside. There was always pot roast, but then screaming over the butcher bill would always be a big deal, too. My siblings and I also apparently had an insatiable desire for hamburgers.

When I was around ten, I made the unfortunate mistake of walking in on them during the weekly Saturday fight. Dad scowled at me, "Get the hell out of here, Jerry. You're too young for this."

In my teenage years it dawned on me one day that Mom wasn't an extreme spender, nor were we children spoiled brats who were consuming endless quantities of food. I also realized—as Dad would pull up in his Cadillac, the only one on our block—that we weren't poor. Suddenly the truth hit me that this was all about Dad's management skills. We kids never talked about it with either of them, and they did stay together. Perhaps it was just the thing to do, but there wasn't much love between them. I've never discussed the Saturday mornings with anyone until now.

A strange thing happened to me a few years ago when I started to make some really good money. I began being short-tempered with my wife every time we were out and she'd want to get something. I'd make comments—which was unlike me—about her lack of understanding that I'd have to pay for that item, usually something minor like a book. "You're never going to read that, anyway. All you do is spend," I complained. I was making more money than I ever had in my life, and I could spend plenty on what I wanted without a single thought, but when my wife did, I considered her a spendthrift.

When she yelled back pretty strongly one day, I realized that I was turning into my father. I couldn't believe it. From that day on, I handed over all the financial responsibilities to my wife. For twenty years now, she has done all the banking and made all the investment decisions—everything. I happily make the money and turn it over to her. I've never balanced a checkbook in my life.

It's funny that Jerry thinks he's beaten his demons, because he hasn't. He believes handing everything over to his wife is a great solution, but he's merely hiding from his issues. His fear of screaming at his wife caused him to completely bow out of a part of their lives in which he should be involved; it shouldn't be his wife's complete responsibility to manage the financial part of their family. She should have a partner in Jerry with whom to make joint decisions, but Jerry has never been able to make himself such a partner. He resisted repeating the control that his father exerted over his mother, but he went all the way to the other extreme: abdicating his role and any participation in decision making. He's done better than his father did, but even in this avoidance he is paying daily tribute to his parents' unfortunate and dysfunctional financial relationship.

Like Jerry, we may try to hide from our feelings and our unconsciously learned behaviors about money, but we need to realize that we have a relationship with it. How we come to own this relationship and what we choose to do with it is so deep and so complicated that we tend to never take a really good, hard look at it. We risk an unhealthy relationship with money, filled with messages we learned in childhood and from the society around us. We may use money to control others, dictating what they should and should not do, and feel justified in our anger toward them about it. We may mismanage the money ourselves, all in attempt to placate an inner voice with which we are not in touch.

Now is as good a time as ever to explore your personal relationship with money and where it comes from.

The Many Voices You Have Within

Gary: I've discussed my theory of inner-voice recognition in my books, but until now I've never specifically related it to money. It seems that everyone has some memory of his or her childhood messages about money. Did Mom lie to Dad about how much things cost? Did your parents fight over money? Did you think you should have stuff that your parents refused to buy? Money is interwoven throughout so many parts of our lives that we all have had to deal with it regularly since childhood.

There are three primary voices in your head: the child voice, the society voice, and the home voice.

Child Voice

The child voice is perhaps the most significant of the three voices, because it is the first, the oldest, and probably the one you drew on and brought to the other two.

Do you remember how young and impressionable you were as a kid? My favorite example is the Mother's Day or Father's Day gift I used to bring my parents—you know, the really ugly thing made in kindergarten class. In my day there was a propensity for all gifts made of papier-mâché, which often meant making your parent an ashtray regardless of whether your parents smoked. I'd busy myself creating some new misshapen object that I would artistically paint green and orange and then present with pride. Of course, I hoped for the obviously perfect response from my parents: "You made this? I can't believe it. It's beautiful." Then I could walk away feeling phenomenal and on top of the world.

Yet it's not true. You and I created junk that our parents couldn't give away to the next-door neighbor. But truth has little to do with forming our minds and our emotions. Our parents could have gotten the present, looked bewildered, and commented, "Well, it's nice and all, but I don't smoke, and I'm not sure where it would go." Hearing that comment, the child would be heartbroken. This reaction all has little to do with the object itself and everything to do with the message a parent chooses to give you at that moment.

I don't believe that one comment like this will make or break a child's emotional well-being for the rest of his or her life. However, millions of comments in one direction or the other will. Our parents gave us message after message about life when we had no choice but to accept their opinions as the laws of life. They usually intended only to help us, but it doesn't mean that they always did.

What could a five-year-old like Jerry possibly think about money other than what his parents taught him? Dad owns it, Mom spends it, and Dad is angry about it. Jerry learned that even if you drive the nicest car in town, you'll still worry about money and fight about it. These are realities that Jerry—and all of us with our own unique messages—absorbed from our upbringing. It's an early imprinting that we continue to follow, most of the time never identifying or seriously considering the

Getting in Touch with Your Childhood Money Messages

Answer the following questions to stimulate your thinking about money:

What were the differences between Mom and Dad in how they handled money?

To whom did the money "belong"?

Who was responsible for making the money?

Who was responsible for managing the money?

How did my parents discuss money with each other?

How did my parents discuss money with me?

What's my earliest childhood memory about money?

What was the relationship between success and money in my childhood home?

What was the relationship of power and control to money in my childhood home?

What was the relationship of beauty and attractiveness to money in my childhood home?

What was the relationship of fun and happiness to money in my childhood home?

By responding to these questions, you'll begin to gain some insight into how you came to understand what money means to you. After answering each question, return to your answers and make a note of how close your answer would fit with your children's answers if they were to do the same activity.

origins of the message. We are merely following our parents' lead in how to live our financial lives.

Our view of money extends beyond earning and spending it. One's personal sense of success, beauty, and self-esteem is tied up with money. Money affects our lives in ways we're not even aware.

I'm always happy when I can help a couple realize that a lot of their behaviors or fears are related to false premises or false thinking. When the message is one we learned as children, it's harder to change, but it's still possible to do so.

If you recognize the money messages you were given as a child and how much those messages affect the way you lead your present financial life, you can reexamine those attitudes to see if they serve your present best interests.

To put your concerns at rest, let's clearly state that this exercise is not meant to judge your parents in any way. We all have loyalty issues, and after all the good that our parents did for us, we're often uncomfortable blaming them for our adult issues. We understand that we need to be responsible for our adult behavior and not excuse it with a "what can I do, look what they did to me" attitude.

If your parents fought over money, you can't judge them for doing so. Who knows what they had to deal with when *they* were children? What we can judge is the impact they had on you as a child.

Society Voice

Let's face it: keeping up with the Joneses is a real issue for a lot of people. We receive countless messages from those around us.

Betje and her partner, Jan, live in Amsterdam. When we went to stay at their new apartment building on the water near the heart of Amsterdam, it was a cultural revelation. The rooms were lovely and comfortably appointed, but there was no bathtub, no dryer, and no humongous subzero freezer. We hung our clothes on the line outside on the balcony, took showers, and shopped for fresh food to put in the little refrigerator each day. Jan had a car, but the rest of the family rode bicycles everywhere, as do many of the Dutch. Our kids stood openmouthed as they looked at the streets filled with thousands of bikes; parents took three kids to school on bicycles with special seats. Everyone looked fit. The cashier at the ice cream store just stared at us when we asked for a sample—there were no samples.

Betje is a social worker, and Jan is a photographer. They work a four-day week and spend Wednesdays with their children, who are off from school that afternoon. We took tremendous pleasure in the slower pace of their lives. We admired the fact that Jan made delicious espresso and that they had the time to enjoy discussions of world events over a quiet cup of coffee. They lived well, we concluded. Their lives were truly richer than those of most people we know.

I was almost embarrassed when they visited us here in the United States and my sister drove up in her big SUV with one baby in it. We went out for ice cream, and the Dutch family said that the four of them could share one sundae. It turned out that they could.

I love our country and our lifestyle, but we are so influenced by marketing. My kids, who are rail thin, were loaded up with bags of pretzels and cookies and other snacks for an outing that would last maybe four hours. They looked ready for a transatlantic crossing.

"Theo has an apple; he will be fine with that," Betje said, not judgmentally. Later on, her son found a water fountain while all the other kids lined up at the soft-drink machine.

When your neighbor decides that purchasing a certain car is the thing to do, or that she should send her kids to the "right" school or invest her money in a certain fund, this all becomes part of the messages we hear. The ads that show certain lifestyles contribute to our concept of what the norm is. We see what others are doing with their money, and unless we have a strong idea of what we personally want to do, their actions will affect the decisions we make in all kinds of ways.

Advertisements and product placements in movies are so aggressive that they conspire to influence how you "should" be living, what clothing you should buy, where you should go on vacation, how you should look, and how your children should dress. These are not public service announcements; they are messages designed to take our money and our life energy with it. We rarely stop to consider whether any of this truly makes us happier. Ask yourself these questions:

- How do my friends and my family affect my relationship with money?
- How do advertisements affect my relationship with money?
- What does mass media teach me about money?
- What would my best friend tell me is the most important thing about money?
- What are my favorite advertisements? Did I purchase any of the items promoted in the ads?

- What's the first thing I notice when I see my friends or my family?

- What does my society tell me about my obligations with money?

- What are my two best friends' relationships to money like?

Review your answers to get a deeper idea of the messages with which society bombards you.

Home Voice

If you have children, they will speak volumes about how you live your financial life. They won't even have to talk. Even as you gaze into your newborn's eyes, you feel as though you're receiving a financial message: feed me, care for me, dress me as nicely as the other kids on the block, let me see the world—you don't want me to regret not seeing the world, do you? We want so much and so many things for those we love that we would seem to be doomed from the start. After all, we can't possibly give our children everything they want, simply because human nature seems to be that the more you get, the more you want.

Consider these questions:

- What does my mate or spouse need financially to have his or her basic needs met?

- What do my children need financially to have their basic needs met?

- Why does my mate want what he or she wants? Is it because society tells my mate to want it, because my mate's family taught it, or because it's the genuine desire of my mate?

- Why do my children want what they want? Is it because their friends have those things? Has society had a hand in convincing your kids that they need them?

By exploring the three inner voices, you'll come to realize that there's a great deal of chatter going on in your head that was largely unrecognizable to you in the past. Once you recognize the voices that are talking to you, you will have more of a level playing field in your head and can start making real choices. Do you want to continue to adopt these voices, or do you want to develop one of your own, based on your personal belief system? If your parents taught you healthy messages about money, there's no reason to fight that voice if it sends you positive messages. That's true for any voice.

More often, however, we carry complicated messages that harm us and those we love. Take control and empower yourself to develop your own money voice. Consider what money should and should not mean to you. Don't continue on a negative path simply because others have shown you that path. Grow into a healthier financial you.

Roberta and Tom's Story: What the Jewelry Really Meant

Roberta and Tom were on the brink of divorce. A highly successful entrepreneur, Tom had borrowed a huge amount of money from lending institutions just before the recession. He lost almost everything. In order to save one of their most important investments, he had to arrange that two very expensive pieces of

Roberta's jewelry be placed as collateral against the loan. Roberta felt terribly betrayed and lost all respect for her husband. She told him that there was nothing worse he could've done, and she let him know how infuriated she was on an almost daily basis. Tom, in turn, was angered by her response. These were pieces he had bought for her when he was doing very well. They were so expensive that they had stayed in the vault, and she had worn each piece only once. He promised her that they wouldn't even have to be sold, and thought she was wrong for being hostile when the jewelry was still sitting in the vault. He expected her to be supportive and was shocked when she wasn't.

They both looked at their inner voices to see more deeply into this dilemma.

Child voice. Tom had always felt that his father didn't accept him. The younger of two sons, Tom considered his older brother, Sam, to be the golden child: the best at sports, the best in school. Sam followed in the footsteps of his father and was groomed to take over Dad's business. Tom didn't follow in his father's footsteps: he didn't finish college, he didn't get an MBA, and he didn't become a business professional like his father and his brother. Tom was successful nonetheless, and with a lot of "hustling," as he referred to it, he made it big. It never seemed to make a difference to his dad, though, who continually seemed to be indifferent to Tom's success.

At the point at which he almost lost it all, Tom had to admit that borrowing money had been a mistake and that he should have known better. Why had he needed so many loans that he even put his wife's jewelry up for hock? When he looked at his childhood voice, he found two themes that had brought him to this uncomfortable place.

First, he realized that no matter how much money he accumulated and how much he owned, it would never be enough, because he was reacting to the "father voice"—the one that said he wasn't accepted. In his father's world, acceptance came with money. That was success. That's all his father did—make money—and he expected his kids to do the same. Even though Tom believed that his father had never accepted him, he was still trying, deep down, to prove to his father, to himself, and to the world that he was indeed a success.

Second, he understood that the loans were a form of acceptance in themselves. With every loan came independent approval from someone who was saying, "We'll bet on you with our money." Tom had forgotten about the time he asked his father for a loan for his first investment and his father had turned him down. Making a name for himself and being able to qualify for outrageous loans made him feel accepted.

Roberta had her own issues with money and childhood. Her father, a salesman, traveled the world; some years he made lots of money, and other years he made almost nothing. As a child she was constantly moving: to a mansion one year, to a simple apartment the next, and to a farm two years later. She used to joke with her mother that she wasn't going to unpack her box of special items because she knew they'd be leaving soon.

Her father died when she was eleven, and she was heartbroken. He had been traveling, and she hadn't seen him for a month. Roberta and her mother moved in with Roberta's sister and her family until Roberta went away to college. Roberta understood that she never truly felt her father's full presence, because he had been so consumed with work. He always sent her trinkets from every exotic place, and he always made sure to bring back jewelry for his wife. Basically, all Roberta had from her father were her trinkets and her mother's jewelry, which would one day be hers. The jewelry was nothing expensive, but it was priceless to her.

Now Roberta understood some deeper things about her present situation. First, she understood why she had freaked out about Tom using her jewelry as collateral. The jewelry meant much more to her than an expensive gift from her husband that she barely wore and hardly ever saw. It represented a love well beyond what Tom ever meant it to be.

Second, she understood how much she hated him for taking out big loans, yet she had been more encouraging about that than she had admitted at first. She was a strong woman, involved in many of Tom's decisions, and she could have requested that he do things differently. She said that deep down she was kind of happy to go along with it.

She had already formed an expectation in childhood, and that voice told her that a money roller coaster was the way to go. Financial stability was never part of her world. She had married and emotionally supported her husband, betting high and riding on another roller coaster.

Now the two of them could discuss a new vision. Tom had to become a man who was not going to find success through lots of money and approval from loan officers at banks. He realized that no amount of money would ever make him feel accepted. He'd always be trying to gain acceptance from a ghost father against whom he couldn't win. He would have to overcome this situation as best as he could and work with his wife to build a nest egg that would not be touched or leveraged.

Roberta was able to reduce her anxiety over her jewelry. Still hoping that it remained hers, she ultimately realized that she was unlikely to lose it and that Tom was working hard to make sure she wouldn't. She had to pull back from the emotional connection she was making between Tom's gifts and the objects she had received from her father. She had to become a partner with Tom.

Society voice. Roberta and Tom lived in a community of very wealthy people. Like themselves, most were self-made and were more than happy to show the world how rich they were. This voice shouted at Tom and Roberta to look wealthy and buy the best of everything. Roberta belonged to a posh spa and to a charitable group where the underlying message was "spend, spend, spend." New fashion was regularly discussed, tennis bracelets were worn to exercise, and considerable donations were made at every charity meeting. Tom went on expensive golf trips with the guys on which private planes and the best scotch were the norm.

Home voice. Roberta and Tom's three children were all under ten. Roberta and Tom believed that their kids were happy just being with their parents. The kids would balk if they had to move, change schools, and give up some friends, but their voice would be to do whatever would make their parents stop fighting and become a happily married couple.

Roberta and Tom used the inner-voice recognition formula to discover some of the deeper reasons their economic woes were hitting them so hard. With their deeper insights, they could use their energy to fix their lives together and get back to being a couple that could still have some fun and find a renewed intimacy. They took away the stumbling blocks to their daunting anger and were able to develop a new way of responding to each other about money and much more.

Roberta and Tom had to recognize that accepting themselves and each other was enough. Love had to be shown through kind gestures, not money. Their collective definition of success had to move out of finances and back to relationships and good experiences. They needed to offer themselves and their children a stable home life. Now they knew the direction they needed to move in, and they had a framework to develop their own voices and not merely give in to impulses drawn from the voices of others.

Julie and Andrew's Story: The Cost of Procrastination

Julie was at her wits' end when the economy tanked. Her life with Andrew was different from that of most couples because neither of their jobs was in jeopardy: she was a nurse-practitioner and he was a tenured college professor. However, they had worked very hard to build a nest egg, and that appeared to be gone. They had a small stock portfolio that was now worth a bit more than the paper the statements came on. They also owned a commercial building and two rental apartments that were in foreclosure.

Two years ago, they had thought about selling the commercial building, and an agent told them they could get a generous offer. Julie believed that they should take the offer and sell the building. She thought it was a good deal, especially since there was already talk of a recession in the media. Andrew agreed, but he never got around to moving forward on it, claiming that he was too busy to deal with all of the paperwork. Shortly thereafter, the conversations about the sale stopped.

Now they were looking at an almost empty building that was heavily mortgaged, which had never been an issue in a decent economy; the building had almost always been filled with stores and offices. As the recession rolled in, however, the building emptied out, and they were not going to be able to keep it. The tenants in their apartments were requesting a few months' leeway in rent, because they had been fired and were now between jobs.

Julie was furious about being in this position. She had repeatedly told Andrew to sell the building, and she reminded him of how different their lives would be if he had followed through with that. Andrew was upset about the situation and felt foolish for missing the opportunities, but didn't think that Julie's anger was reasonable. He had always seen Julie as a complete partner. He hated it when she played the "little housewife" and left financial matters to him after dictating what she thought he should do with their finances. The tension was high, and they barely talked anymore. Their two teenagers were out of the house with their friends more and more. Julie and Andrew didn't have any plans to divorce, but this crisis clearly activated a lot of hostility in their marriage.

They both looked at their inner voices to see more deeply into this dilemma.

Child voice. Julie's mother was hard-working and loving, and she took complete care of the home and of Julie and her three sisters. Julie's father was an alcoholic and a gambler, so whatever money he made was spent very haphazardly. Julie's mother never stopped putting Julie's father down, and she constantly argued with him about his lack of financial support.

Julie was given the message that a woman had better take care of herself. Her mother had dropped out of high school when she was pregnant with her first baby. She worked her way up through the system and eventually made decent money managing a doctor's office. Julie realized for years that the reason she became a nurse-practitioner was to be self-supporting, if necessary, and to never have to be dependent on a man. Her dad had failed her mom, and she was angry at him for that.

As she considered all of this, she also realized that she had a pattern of trying to make Andrew into the financial controller of the family. She admitted to herself and to Andrew that even though she could do much more for the family financially, such as arranging for the sale of the building herself or as a partner with Andrew, she would lose respect for him if that happened. She was caught up in anger at her father and was still drawing on that to try to coax Andrew into being a "real man," in full control of the family finances.

However, from the day she had met Andrew at Berkeley, she had known that he was not an aggressive businessman and had never planned to make a great deal of money. His love of literature drove his desire to teach. He wanted to let Julie take care of the money, but she had refused, and any time he wanted to do anything, she obeyed reluctantly. She'd ask him for money for food shopping, and he'd tell her to get it from the bank. She'd ask how much, and he'd respond with how should he know? Then she would become angry that he wasn't more in charge of it all, and he would wonder what she was so angry about.

Andrew's father had taken complete control of the family finances and had made a great living. Andrew grew up experiencing a dazzling lifestyle filled with the good things in life—that is, until his father left his mother for a younger woman who worked at the office with him. Then Andrew, his mother, and his younger sister had nothing. Andrew's lifestyle changed overnight. Mom had nothing in her name, and Dad had been able to hide his fortune in ways that his mother was unable and too weak to find. She had taken the deal he had offered her, trusting that he'd always take care of her and the children. It proved to be a big financial mistake.

Andrew was hurt by his father and spent his adolescence and beyond expressing anger to anyone who'd listen. What he didn't realize was how much anger he still had with his mother for placing complete trust in her husband. When Andrew's father left her, she didn't know the first thing about finances, and she completely fell apart. There were years when she barely kept them afloat.

Yet Andrew was also grateful to his mother and loved her a lot, so it was easier to displace much of his anger onto his wife. Once he began talking about those years, he could see that he had been angry and frustrated. If only his mother had been more aware of things and a bit less trusting, she could have saved herself and her family so much grief. He realized that she had done the best she could and that his father had, after all, abandoned the family. All that anger was affecting his present life.

The last thing Andrew wanted was to be the boss in the relationship. He had learned very early that money wasn't all it was cracked up to be, and he wanted a life in which he was able to do what he loved to do. Teaching gave him that opportunity, and he married a smart woman who made more money than he did for most of their married life. He took pride in his wife's awareness of finance. He was angry when she tried to make him do everything for the family's finances.

The mix was explosive. Julie's voice told her to make her man financially responsible, whereas Andrew's voice shouted for him to make his wife financially aware. These voices led them to become angrier and more distant from each other.

Society voice. Julie and Andrew lived in a college community. Their friends, mostly professors and health-care workers, tended to be regimented and frugal. Nobody felt the need to be flashy, and there was never any pressure to impress others. This voice told them to be satisfied with what they have, to feel blessed that their jobs were not in jeopardy, and to continue loving each other.

Home voice. Julie and Andrew had two teenagers who were locked into a moneyed society. One of the perks of Andrew's profession was that he could send his kids to an outstanding prep school in the area, so they were going to school with the children of the superwealthy. Julie and Andrew's kids saw something alluring in that lifestyle, and their voice encouraged a concern with money and a commitment to keeping the goodies coming.

Julie and Andrew grew a great deal through their deeper insight. Their childhood voices caused them to react harshly to their financial situation, and this became evident to them only when the recession hit. They faced the truth: money was always a sore spot for them, even when they had plenty and were doing well with their investments. There was still a lot of eye rolling and bickering over control of the money. Their arguments weren't about each one trying to control the money, but just the opposite: each was trying to get the other one to take control. The intensity of their anger and their loss of respect for each other because neither wanted control of the finances came from their deeper childhood issues.

Julie and Andrew confronted the fact that they'd contributed to a lifestyle for their children that they personally didn't want or need. They decided to take their children on charitable outings or trips as a way to help them change their inner voices about money.

Julie and Andrew realized that they had landed in the perfect spot in their community. They enjoyed friends who were of like mind, and wanted this voice to be their primary one. With their anger reduced and their issues realized, they followed the lead of their friends and developed a cooperative plan for managing their financial lifestyle.

Choosing Your Voices

It's shocking to consider how much our emotions are affected by the messages sent to us by others. If you've never considered your belief system and have just adopted it without any adult thought, then you could be said to be living someone else's life.

That doesn't mean you have to challenge everything your parents, your society, or your home life have ever taught you. If there are parts of these messages that work well for you, you might never even want to consider where they came from and instead just thank your lucky stars that you have what works for you.

However, your upbringing might have given you certain messages that have no real application in your life now. Perhaps your school put you in the C class with all the less-than-smart kids, and you came to believe that you weren't so bright. Perhaps your parents were angry people who were hypercritical, making you believe that you were incapable. Maybe you've been fulfilling the voice of messing things up because that's what you came to expect from yourself, and you don't even know it. You just keep making poor judgments and proving to yourself how incapable you are.

We live our best lives when we encourage ourselves to rethink the messages of our inner voices and decide today whether we like them, whether we wish to subscribe to them, and whether we will ditch them and create our own new voices. You can create a new voice with daily care and attention to how you are acting. It may at first feel uncomfortable to place so much focus inside yourself, but within a couple of weeks you'll see immense changes and begin to feel a newfound freedom from old voices. The voices that build you up and make you feel good about yourself, your love, and your future are keepers.

Remember that your family and your society have their own agendas. Many parents send negative messages to their children and don't mean to do so. They wish their children wouldn't take their own parental weaknesses personally. Sometimes parents are just not at their best due to life circumstances, and they can't be there for their children at a critical time. The children are likely to take that personally and define themselves based on it.

Whatever your experience was, look deeply within yourself and change your perspective. You can give yourself the power and the courage to change your life for the better, in good times and bad.

6

Attack the Problem, Not Each Other

There's nothing like feeling part of a team. When my kids interviewed the tennis star Roger Federer for their sports column and video, they asked him to name one of his greatest struggles as a tennis player. He answered that not being on a team has its drawbacks. In fact, he most missed being part of a team when he won a tournament. He explained that when you win, you want to jump into other people's arms and celebrate, and as a single player on a court you just stand around by yourself.

Teamwork is at the root of almost every successful system, whether it's in sports, business, or religion. Every relationship is a team if both partners choose to make it one. Failed couples have a pattern of quickly judging and blaming the other and feeling resentful about being the victim. Each partner attacks the other, and their valuable energy is wasted because attacking and belittling doesn't usually result in a real apology or understanding. Their energy is exhausted by the personal attack, so by the time the attack is over, there is no energy left over for a healthy discussion about how to deal with the issue.

Teamwork Is at the Root of Successful Couples

Successful couples sees themselves as a team whether the partners are aware of it or not. They don't resent each other when one or the other has to pick up the slack. There's an inherent trust that neither will take advantage of the other. There's an understood rule of sacrifice, but it goes both ways, and each partner expects appreciation for his or her efforts. In past generations there was an understanding in some marriages that the wife would work while the husband finished school, at which point she'd stop working and raise the children while he became the primary wage earner. In today's terms, that understanding could mean anything from cooking dinner and balancing the checkbook when your spouse has the flu to getting up in the middle of the night to soothe a baby because your spouse is exhausted. The inherent team rule is that neither person wants to impose on the other and would do everything in his or her power to avoid that.

Gary: I am a night person and was generally on the "night awareness" duty when our children were small, so if I wasn't getting up in the night for some reason, Melisa knew I must be exhausted. Similarly, if she, the morning person, was not getting up early, then I knew she must be exhausted. We never considered that one was just lying there thinking that the other one would take care of whatever came up. We are a team. We were not looking to impose on each other.

I never thought that Melisa would take advantage of my working long, intense hours by spending her days ignoring our children and caring only for herself. I was happy when she would take a break to enjoy herself and avoid becoming overtired or burned out from the demanding schedule of motherhood. I encouraged her to take more time for herself. Likewise, Melisa has always encouraged me to take time off from work so that I could spend it with our family and on my learning or other interests.

Focus on Your Goals

A team has amazing power. Every relationship can harness this intensity by never seeking to blame the other person and instead looking for solutions. The number one way to get through any bad time is to work together and use your collective energy to solve, solve, solve.

I've learned many wonderful things from Melisa. One of the most significant lessons she has taught me is to focus on solutions. Melisa modeled a working tool for reaching a goal. It's quite simple:

1. What do you want to see happen?
2. What is the goal of this?

We often become bogged down in the path that we expected or wanted to take to reach our goal. The path may not be available, but that doesn't mean that we have to do away with the goal. There are always many paths to the same goal, but we get stuck on following the path we're on.

I always wanted to be a rabbi and have a synagogue. When achieving that goal wasn't working for me, Melisa and I sat down, and she asked me to think about what I wanted. I told her, "I want to be a rabbi—always have, always will. I have to figure out how to make this work." We can't just toss our dreams away once we find out that they weren't what we expected, so this is a good technique to use to find alternate ways of making things work better.

After we tried several creative ideas and I still felt unhappy and unfulfilled as a rabbi, Melisa helped me to focus on my goal. Why did I want to be a rabbi? What part of the job did I like? The answer was obvious to both of us: I wanted to help people. Ever since I was little, I had thought that the way to do it was by serving a community as a clergyman. I had never considered that I could help people outside a spiritual community, but Melisa and I started to think about other meaningful ways in which I could help people outside of that particular context.

Reaching this new goal required a shift in my thinking and the willingness to live a different life financially. It would have been easier to just resign myself to being unhappy and continuing in my chosen field, but my unhappiness was impairing my ability to help others as I became more burdened by it all.

I believe that God has to take into account many more things than my own desires. Everything has to interlock. He has to get me where He wants me. So I'll focus on my goal, the deep desire that He's placed within me, and I'll do my best to get there. He will intercede and let me know whether I have to find an alternate route, showing me that I'm needed in a different way. I offer up the ideas, run with them, and, depending on the success of it, maintain them or look to another path through which to achieve my goal of helping people.

I can't begin to count the number of people who have come into my life and allowed me the honor of helping them, people who would not have crossed my path had I remained a small-town rabbi. Who knows why I had to serve one way or the other? I've learned not to get stuck on the path. This form of creative thinking is an important key to getting through bad times.

People usually become frustrated when they lose a job and can't find a new one. They usually look for the exact same job

The Six Best Ways to Solve Your Problems

1. Discuss how you wish things had turned out.
2. Outline the way you wanted to reach your goal.
3. Talk only about what your goal is.
4. Explore every other possible way to reach this goal than the way you've been trying.
5. Decide which new, creative paths seem most likely to get you to this goal.
6. Begin putting all your energy into that new path while keeping yourself open to every other path that could get you to your goal.

over and over again instead of finding an alternate path. When one path isn't working, reduce your issue to the goal instead. One manager at a national chain retail store became incredibly frustrated when she went to sixteen interviews for managing everything from stores to doctors' offices and didn't get a job. She was at a loss for what to do, until she considered her goal of making money and enjoying her job at the same time. That opened a lot of creative doors to her. She approached a high school and offered to teach an advanced placement course on management for college credit and then started giving evening adult education courses on the same topic. She ended up with a lifestyle that afforded her quiet time to write and enjoy herself more.

A couple was losing their house to foreclosure. In their sixties and retired, they didn't want to move in with their children. Going back into the workforce was daunting, and they exhausted themselves trying to find jobs. They had enough money to live on but not to pay a lot for rent or a mortgage. They found house-sitting information on the Internet and began living rent-free in other people's vacation homes. They now occupy one family's two residences and are paid for it as well. It's true that they are occupying the homes during poor weather, in the months that the owners are avoiding the homes, but they are happy not to be back in the workforce.

One single mother lost her job and could no longer afford rent. She had a little savings, just enough to buy an old used boat with a cabin, so she did. It sounds crazy and impulsive, but it's not; if you live in certain places that allow free docking in bay water, all you need is a boat. It had its complications, but she made it work; her two children, ages fourteen and ten, found it adventurous; and it lasted eight months, until she found work that paid her enough to be able to afford rent. She eventually sold the boat for slightly more than she paid for it to somebody who loved her idea of free living in the bay.

Instead of spending money for babysitters, swap babysitting nights with a friend so that both couples can have a date night with no babysitting fees. Share books in a book club and use the library. Libraries offer much more than books: computers, Internet access, the daily newspaper, and a calm, quiet atmosphere in which to focus on them.

If you're not sending your children to the private school of your choice, find alternate ways to get them the education you think they'll be missing. Find online help, perhaps a camp experience in the area, or a friend who can offer help. Barter with friends—each of you often has knowledge that the other doesn't and that your children could use. Share the costs of a private enrichment tutor or enlist a relative with expertise in a field.

There is no end to the creative solutions we can employ. We all know how much work goes into every struggle. Your hard work should at least be directed toward solutions and reaching your goal instead of being wasted on anger, blame, and trying to force yourself onto a path that isn't available or isn't working for you anymore. There is always another creative answer when you let go of the path you had planned on taking.

Finding Creativity: Going Outside Yourself

No one truly does anything on his or her own. We come into this world as dependent beings and need to be connected to others.

None of us can say that he or she did it all without anyone's help. We need others in big ways and small in order to have money, family, love, and life itself. It is helpful to keep this idea in mind when we are searching for creativity.

When the economy is difficult, many of us are forced to start thinking of new ideas for securing our jobs, creating new ones, or developing alternate plans for income. There is a tendency to become lonely in your thoughts, to go into yourself when you are dealing with the hardships of a financial (or any other) struggle. Yet the key to finding new opportunities with creative thinking is to get out and see what everyone else is doing.

Imagine yourself sitting in a room for ten hours straight trying to think of new ways to create income. Now imagine spend-

Go from "I Can't" to "How Can I?" to "I Can"

It's easy to say "I can't." When you can't, then you don't have to take action, because you have failed and know that you will fail again only if you try.

When you feel this way, catch yourself and say "How can I?" What can I do, to whom can I speak, where can I do research, and how do I get help?

Then tell yourself "I can." As you search for ideas, support, and information, more ideas and support come to you. Realize that we all use things outside ourselves to succeed.

ing five of those hours talking to others about what they are doing, searching online for the newest ideas happening in your field of interest or expertise, discussing a partnership with a friend, or listing your ideas aloud to your spouse and hearing feedback. In these scenarios, many minds are working for you, because every idea brings you to a newer place that you would not have considered before. When you discuss with and learn from others, it stimulates your resourceful brain, allowing new ideas to form.

Gary: I created the Sandcastles Program, a three-and-a-half-hour course for children of divorce in four different age groups, and it now operates throughout the world. In terms of helping people, it is the greatest achievement of my professional career. More than two hundred thousand children have completed this program internationally. From it came my first major book, *Helping Your Kids Cope with Divorce the Sandcastles Way*, the subject of at least five segments I've done on *The Oprah Winfrey Show*. Clearly, it has been an important part of my life and my career. How did I come up with the idea?

When I made my move from rabbi to counselor, I had already been doing home studies for the courts in the area of custody arrangements for families going through divorce. The idea of mandating parents to go to a four-hour parenting course before granting them a divorce had begun in other counties, and I volunteered to write one for Miami at no cost. When I put that into effect, the idea dawned on me that what we really need is to provide help directly to the children. Thus the Sandcastles Program was born—I developed it and offered it as part of my private practice work to the county at no cost.

In this case, my goal wasn't to make money but to help people. Yet the enterprise did eventually lead to profit. I never would have developed this worldwide niche unless I had been in the right place at the right time. I only knew about a need as I learned more about court systems and what they were on the cusp of doing. I couldn't have convinced the chief judge, Leonard Rivkind, unless he'd been personally familiar with me and had seen the success the county had had with the mandated parenting program that I had developed.

Fight the urge to stay inside yourself, and start talking to others. Find a cause to give to and improve. Go online and find out what's going on outside you. Find parts of systems or ideas that speak to you, that you believe you can use to fill a space, in which you can develop an expertise. You might find yourself in a whole different area of work than you expected, but you'll be on your feet and advancing. Every second you stay within yourself, you keep building the negative momentum of feeling down, lost, and angry at the world. Every second you go outside yourself, you keep building positive momentum, a forward motion of hope and confidence that one thing will lead to another. If your eyes are wide open, they will see opportunities.

Why Can't He at Least Help More with the Kids?

In the recent recession, the majority of jobs that have been lost are ones that have traditionally been held by men. Now many more women than ever are the primary wage earners. Women may be confused when they see their husbands quickly slide into depression and when they see his inability to regroup.

Society still creates the image that a man is largely responsible for his family's finances. Many, many women have powerful positions in the workplace, in politics, and in most other areas of life, but men are quicker to define themselves by what they "do" for a living. This tendency can understandably cause problems when a man loses his job. He may have believed that he was vital to the company or the system and that he made important contributions to it, so he's shocked when the system or business has no more room for him. If he moves to a job in another field earning the same money, it can still be difficult for him, because he will have come to equate his identity, on some level, with the position he held before. In part, this is why it's complicated for men to simply help out more at home cleaning, cooking, and caring for the children. Men will do it if they're alone or if they have to, but they rarely take an active interest in doing it well or initiating it. A woman is right to expect her partner's help, because that is part of teamwork and of focusing on the goal instead of the path.

Boys in our society must be taught to define themselves more by the differences they can make in society helping others, by their relationships, and by the other truly important things in life, rather than by their job titles and status.

Men: When you are on your deathbed, nobody will be talking about how much money you made. The cash won't crowd around you, making you feel warm and fuzzy. All that will matter is the love you have in your lives, how you've reached out and connected to others, how you've helped and been helped as part of a family and a society. Your job is important, but only as a means to an end. Having money makes things easier, but

Changing Definitions

If you introduce yourself to a newcomer and ask what he or she does, you are likely to get two different answers depending on the sex of the person. A man is more likely to first state what he does for a living: "I'm a doctor, a contractor, a realtor, a business owner, or a manager in a government position." It's also probably going to be his *only* response.

Ask a woman the same question, and she will usually answer that she is a mother and/or is married, if she is either or both. She might say this first or after describing her job. A man sees his living as an end in itself, whereas a woman will more commonly see it as a means to an end. This may be why men tend to do less at home than they should.

beyond filling the basic needs, it doesn't make you happy. The idea is to try to stay positive and look forward to finding new ways to succeed. Look forward to creating income to provide for what's important. Stop feeling guilty about not making more money or not supporting the family at this time. Give your partner support, express appreciation, initiate child-care and household chores, or (if possible) find a service to occasionally do the housecleaning in order to take pressure off both of you. Make it a priority to show your wife that you love her.

Marlene's Story: When the Wife Becomes the Breadwinner

My husband has been out of a job for months now. He's been a builder for years, and the well has dried up a bit lately. He just sits around all day. He is slowly starting a small business but has plenty of free time. I'm a teacher, and I never thought I'd be making the money in the family. I'm okay with it, though. I don't think he did anything wrong.

However, I did expect him to at least be more helpful to me in the home. When he was working, he came home exhausted, which I understood. His job was really labor-intensive. But now he could help me so much around the house. When I return from work, he's in a daze. I've told him I think he's depressed, but he's too proud to agree.

Another thing I don't get is how he still thinks it's his money. For years when he made money, he made only a little more than I did. When it came to spending it, however, he felt like it was his own. He even invested in a friend's startup company and didn't ask me if I thought it was a good idea. I got over it because it turned out to make us a little money. But now that I'm making all of the family money, I don't seem to have the same control over finances that he did when he had his job. It's not that I really want to feel completely in control, but why wouldn't he give me the same courtesy I gave him?

Dave and Karen's Story: Cooking as Therapy

Dave and Karen had been married for thirty-one years when Dave had his hours cut at work. In his new free time he usually surfed the Internet or spent time with his friends. One day he decided to take over the cooking. His wife, Karen, had never liked cooking, and Dave was surprised to find that he enjoyed it and was good at it. He was even more surprised by his wife's genuine delight in coming home to a delicious hot meal, and he built on that. She was working more hours than ever, and he made a special effort to have fun creating good meals served on their fine china. Karen would visibly relax as she came in the door and saw the beautifully set table complete with wine glasses. She told her friends, who agreed it was unusual and very nice to have a husband who did all this.

Dave's mother had died that year, and he went through her old recipe books, making the dishes he'd enjoyed as a child. He enjoyed the familiar smells and flavors from childhood that he hadn't thought about in many years. Some of the dishes were good; a few weren't. Karen didn't criticize him when his efforts floundered. She didn't bring up their financial stress while they ate, she just let herself be nurtured a little, and she really enjoyed it. Dave had found a way to simultaneously contribute to their life in an important way, remember his mother, and make his wife feel loved when she came home after working so hard.

Gary: When Karen told me about Dave's new hobby and how it made them feel romantic, I was very touched. That he could come out of his own space and think about doing something for Karen was wonderful enough. Then, seeing her delight, he took it to another level. It's unusual, because for many men, the devastation that comes with their perceived failure is something they can't even articulate.

Our friend Ted lost a great deal of money in the stock market, and his wife was brilliantly supportive. She told me that he needed to hear her say that it was okay, that she didn't need a lot to get by, and that they'd be happy together no matter what.

Most women I know are strong partners in their relationships regardless of whether they contribute financially to the partnership. So I feel comfortable saying to women that if your partner is a man, he might feel especially threatened and in need of some emotional shoring up if he's feeling primarily responsible in the financial crisis. Being positive and reassuring and avoiding anything negative or emasculating seems like basic kindness, if nothing else. But I'm a little scared to go there.

Melisa: Did you see what happened to Gary on the *Oprah* episode about his book *The Truth about Cheating: Why Men Stray and What You Can Do to Prevent It*? One blogger wrote, "I'm surprised Gary Neuman got out of the studio alive. Those women were furious." I was really surprised, because Gary is a big feminist. I know that people will say I'm biased, however.

Gary's research indicated that feeling a lack of appreciation and kindness at home played a significant role in men's deciding to cheat on their wives, and these findings infuriated some women. They seemed to think that Gary was holding them responsible for their husbands' cheating. That was never Gary's point. In fact, he went to great lengths to help cheaters take responsibility for their behavior. He even wrote a book about it, called *Emotional Infidelity*. Still, so many women were angered by the idea that there might be reasons for a guy's wrong behavior. One audience member told Oprah she didn't have time to be "nice" to her husband.

When a *Miami Herald* reporter asked me if I "follow Gary's ideas," I said, "What? To be kind? To be sensitive to a guy because he has feelings? Yes, I agree with that. To not roll your eyes at your friends and put down his taste in jewelry when he gives you a gift? Yes, I think that's good manners and caring, and that belongs in a relationship."

I wonder why so many of us still expect men to be impervious to put-downs or a lack of support. Many of us demand true equality in our relationships but then become angry when our husbands aren't serving as the main breadwinners. Constantly reevaluating the roles we play as our marriages progress is the key to maintaining the equal partnership we say we want. If a man isn't returning your respect and appreciation, then get help or don't stay in the relationship. Otherwise, he deserves basic respect *and* your appreciation.

People in thirty- and forty-year marriages have told me that *The Truth about Cheating*—and the chapters on sexual intimacy and appreciation, in particular—improved their relationships in ways they hadn't thought possible.

It is important to be supportive of each other in any way possible and to acknowledge the feelings you might have about your new responsibilities. Ultimately, it's about finding ways of being there for each other when our place in the world feels shaky.

7

How to Discuss Money in Relationships

In a lot of households, a financial meeting begins when some-one—often the guy—steps out of a room waving a credit card statement or a bill and either quietly or loudly calls on the gods of the universe to explain why shoes, sheets, golf clubs, iPhone apps, and the like are so expensive. How could this be? The other party murmurs understanding, utters a few soothing words, claims not to be responsible for the purchases, or goes on the attack and makes comments about how their friends live. There might then be mutual hand-wringing and a promise to do better. Soon, very soon.

The problem with this approach is that it doesn't solve any-thing. It shuts down the money dialogue even when there isn't a fight, and it creates tiny tears in the fabric of the relationship because each partner goes away feeling bad.

For years it didn't seem to matter; credit was flowing. For many people there was always available cash and capital, refinancing strategies, and all manner of creative lending. Now not so much. No matter who you are, from the loftiest financier to the those without a dime, everyone needs a money dialogue as part of his or her relationship. There is stress in keeping your thoughts and concerns to yourself. *Sharing your stress usually alleviates your stress.* The benefits of talking directly are great, yet we often don't even want to start.

Why We Avoid Financial Discussions

In order to really start the dialogue, we have to understand our resistance to it. Spending activates the pleasure centers of our brains. Gathering and acquiring are hardwired into our brains so that we can survive famine and the invading armies. There is no biological impetus that compels us to review our credit card statements or evaluate our finances. For that reason, we think it's a good idea to serve chocolate at your meeting. If you'd like to unlink pleasure and food (good luck with that one), then instead of serving chocolate you might consider having your meeting and then going out for a walk or to exercise—anything that links the financial discussion experience with something pleasurable.

Liz's Story: Spending Influences

Liz spent her childhood listening to her father talk about living for the moment. "Carpe diem," he would say. A tall man with a booming laugh and a white Hemingwayesque beard, he loved life, and spending money was always fun for him. His own father had died in middle age, and his brothers went off to war, so his worldview became "Spend today, because you don't know about tomorrow." Nevertheless, his idea of carpe diem was mostly limited to the stuff he could afford: an extra pie at the bakery or name-brand bicycles for the girls. He never mentioned that a nice portion of his income went to savings, a little piece of land over here, and a partial ownership of something else over there. He talked a lot about how much fun it was to spend, but he never talked much about saving. Liz received a partial message.

Liz bought things all the time. Her purchases were all designer items whose costs far exceeded what she could afford. When she thought about the childhood messages she had received, she realized that she was trying to re-create the joy of being with her dad, when he would buy her things. She needed to gain some control and find other ways of feeling nurtured.

Once you understand the early messages you received, you can counter their power by staying aware of them. Ask yourself,

Do I need the best brand of this item, or will a less expensive version meet my needs?

If your partner constantly uses money to control or withhold love, why would you want to meet and discuss the topic? We all know that discussion can't end well. If your partner is crazy or irrational in his or her spending, a meeting can be a dead end. He or she will insist that it was a good idea to have the concept artist come in and paint the bathroom for five grand. In those cases you may choose to have the meeting with an objective and respected third party. A marriage counselor, a clergyman, or an accountant can help you to address your desire to see the whole picture.

People whose spending is completely inappropriate are exhausting to deal with. They deny that there is even a problem, all evidence to the contrary. They can hold responsible positions, and they may appear to have it all under control, but the reality can be very different. The partners of such people often have to deal with that disconnect, and it can be frustrating, to say the least. If your partner is one of these people, recognizing it can save you heartache and financial ruin. These people won't discuss or disclose all the financial information, and their "solutions" are punitive, such as "Fine, we'll stop spending. I'm taking the kids out of their school and canceling the cleaning help."

People like this can make you uncomfortable, asking you to open credit cards in your name, sign loans, and give them total financial power in the name of "trusting" them. There is an old saying: "Trust everyone, especially the untrustworthy." That is, trust the untrustworthy to be what they have shown themselves to be: untrustworthy. If your partner has lied about important financial information and has been untrustworthy in the past, trust that this is how he or she will be in the future. Insist on financial oversight. Now is the time for more conversation, not less.

Janet's Story: **Where Did the Money Go?**

Janet, a respected attorney, was married to Richard. She stopped working to care for the couple's two boys, ages eight and six.

"When I stopped working it wasn't an issue, because Richard was an investment banker [at the time a respected and lucrative position] and there was enough money," she said—except that there really wasn't. There never seemed to be enough.

"He was always saying things like 'You need to sign this because we need another loan on the home equity' and blah blah blah. He'd leave with a bunch of documents and I'd wonder, 'What's going on? Where did the money go?' I wondered if he had a gambling addiction or a whole other family he was supporting. I really did."

The truth was that Richard was just a big spender. Janet remembers him coming home with two cars, one for her and one for him. "He liked this feeling of, 'Hey, I don't even have to ask what it costs. Give me one, and one for the missus.' And what? You think I didn't like it when he brought home cars and expensive jewelry? It was nice, and he seemed to be doing well; we could afford it." But, actually, they couldn't afford it. Janet recounted how shocked she was when she discovered that Richard had been raiding their retirement accounts.

Then she found out that he'd made donations. "Oh, that was the best," she said sarcastically. "He pledged unbelievable amounts to charities his friends ran—excuse me? His friends have a charity event, and he gives them our money for strangers? What about us? Charity begins at home."

Richard wasn't evil, and he wasn't purposely ruining the family, a marriage therapist explained. He was delusional in his childlike aspirations to keep up with and even surpass his friends in a wealthy and popular lifestyle. He had just gotten in over his head.

Janet was unusual in that she recognized the problem before it took over their lives, and she acted quickly. "I think I was also willing to lose him," she confesses. "I grew up with a father who drank too much and just couldn't be there for my mom and the kids. To me this was even worse. I told Richard that either this changes or I'm leaving. That did it. We went for help, and we stopped spending. Richard actually did have some impulsivity and depression issues that he never wanted to deal with, and he went on medication for a while. Ultimately I think he knew that he would lose me, so he went along with it."

Systematic Desensitization: Changing Your Reactions to Finances

The psychological behavioral technique known as systematic desensitization—changing your associations to something and overcoming your fear of it—is applied by some to the area of financial awareness. Because some people have such negative associations with bills and paperwork, they become tense or fearful just at the thought of them. Many people avoid thinking about them entirely, leading to obvious problems.

Denise practically hyperventilated every time she saw the stack of bills on her desk. She saw an article on systematic desensitization, and when she walked by the pile of papers, she breathed deeply and visualized something pleasant. The next day she breathed again, but she knew that all that breathing and visualizing wasn't really enough. So she started small, dealing with one envelope and talking on the phone with a friend while she wrote a check. She created positive experiences around each new encounter with finances.

The next day she played some music she loves while she organized her paperwork and checked her balances. Each time,

Systematic Desensitization

Systematic desensitization helps people to change their fearful associations and to approach situations they tend to avoid. Use good visualizations and deep breathing when you think about the tasks you need to do, such as paying bills and dealing with other financial paperwork. Then pair the bill paying with a positive association, such as music. Use small successes to create a new attitude toward the task.

101

she set herself up for a more comfortable association, and with each step she felt a little more relaxed. When she became over-whelmed, instead of throwing the whole pile of bills into a drawer, she would call her well-organized aunt and ask if she could stop by for coffee and a planning session. These new associations helped her to tackle the problems rather than just hand them over to someone or deny them.

Setting Up Your Financial Meeting

Like any good working system, a weekly financial meeting will help you keep on top of things and maintain healthy communication and a feeling of cooperation. Create a consistent time that works for both of you (never late at night) and limit the meeting so that you both know it can't go on forever. Typically, setting a half hour is workable and knowing the limit is there will also keep both of you focused on the goal of dealing with the issues instead of allowing the meeting to spill over into the rest of your day. You may choose to meet more than once a week, but if you do, limit the meeting length and set the time in advance so each of you can be prepared.

1. Set a time that is mutually beneficial. People who are not night people won't want to talk about potentially stressful topics as they're going to bed. Don't meet when one of you is hungry, sleep-deprived, or very out of sorts. Set yourself up for successful communication.

2. If your surroundings affect your mood, choose a room that's quiet and pleasant or go to a location that makes you

feel neutral, like the library or an office. Gather all credit card statements, bills, and banking transactions or view them online. The important thing is that you get a total picture of what's going on.

3. The meeting should be held in a spirit of teamwork and kindness. Agree to avoid blaming, assigning guilt, and making any digs or petulant remarks. If one person has little self-control or there are other issues in the marriage, enlist the help of a respected third party. Consumer credit counseling services are free. Marriage therapists are not just for crazy people in crummy marriages. Smart couples get counseling, and having just one or two sessions to go over finances can bring relief.

4. Avoid statements that begin with *you*. Use ones that start with *I*. This is an old technique, but it works. Instead of "You decided to upgrade the computers, so here's yet another exorbitant charge for that," try "I would like in the future to talk about big electronics upgrades before we do them." Say "I feel overwhelmed by these office expenses" instead of "Your office expenses are ridiculous." The messages are kinder, come across as less accusatory, and forestall defensive arguments. They spare feelings and communicate the importance of finding solutions. It's a win-win dynamic as opposed to your winning at your partner's expense.

5. If you're stressed, breathe slowly and deeply. New brain imaging technology shows that brain patterns actually change when relaxation begins with slow deep breathing. Drink water, not alcohol, because alcohol lowers inhibitions

and can change the tone of the meeting. Have a drink together afterward if that appeals to you.

6. A spirit of friendliness works well. Compliment your partner. Touch each other. Both lower anxiety. Avoid pointing out things that make your partner ashamed.

Guidelines for a Weekly Financial Meeting

- Set a time that appeals to both of you.
- Choose a calming setting.
- Minimize distractions. Turn off your cell phone or set it to vibrate, put on a movie for the kids or ask someone to babysit for a little while, and make sure the pets have been taken care of.
- Connect the discussion to something pleasurable. Serve something good to eat or follow the meeting with a walk, a movie, or another enjoyable activity.
- Set a time limit and adhere to the schedule. A half hour is a good start.
- Bring all materials: your bank statements, information on everything financial.
- Set up computers, complete with any software programs you use (such as Quicken), or a pad of paper and a pen ahead of time.
- Be kind and supportive. Use "I" messages, and avoid accusing and shaming.

One woman told someone at a barbecue that her husband had been fired. He had been upset and ashamed about the recent job loss, even though it wasn't tied to his performance, and had asked her not to mention it. Yet here she was, talking to her friends about why she was working longer hours and how angry she was. Later she told him not to make a big deal about it, that she was "just playing around and forgot." This was part of their style; they often put each other down and rarely apologized or became more careful.

If your style as a couple involves judging and shaming each other, you will have to agree that it can't continue. It's counterproductive, because shame and humiliation don't belong in a relationship, and they definitely don't bring about change.

7. Stick to practical matters, be reassuring to each other, and build each other up. A financial discussion is not the place to review personality defects or air other grievances.

8. Brainstorm ideas on paper. Make lists. Ask questions like ones below, then split up information gathering to get the answers.

   - Can we lower the insurance bills?
   - Who can we call to discuss insurance options?
   - Is there a better way to structure the loan?
   - Are there government programs to help with tuition?

9. Ask family members and friends for information when that is helpful.

   In her best-selling book *Nickel and Dimed: On (Not)*

Getting By in America, Barbara Ehrenreich went undercover to live on minimum wage and explore the lives of those who struggle to get by. One of the most interesting things she found is the sociological impact of culture on information gathering as it pertains to finances.

Some cultures, Ehrenreich writes, share personal information. Latino families know how much the sister-in-law is making, where she works, and the details of her job. Some other cultures don't share to that extent, and they simply don't ask personal questions. As a result, they won't know, for example, that the place a block away is hiring for double what they are being paid.

10. The purpose of a weekly financial meeting is not just to go over the bills, although you'll want to do that. It's to examine how you're going about things. Ask yourselves the following: Are we getting the maximum for our efforts? Are we thinking outside the box and challenging ingrained cultural assumptions and familiar comfort zones?

Creating a Budget

"Who is wealthy?" the Talmud asks. "He who is happy with his lot." Well yes, but isn't it human nature to want your lot to expand a little more? It's what we do. It's why we talk on cell phones instead of landlines tethered to the wall. We like more. You might be happy with your closet, but there's always room for one more pair of shoes or pants. We always want the next electronic life enhancer, a vacation, or tickets to something. Even if you have eliminated extras in your life, there will be things that you decide you need, like braces for your kids' teeth.

That's why budgets don't work. They're like the cabbage soup diet: eventually you have to eat more than cabbage soup all day. We can make vows to spend only on essentials, but after a short time we will want to or have to spend money. Money is a part of normal life. Deciding where it goes and what we get in return for it can be an enormous challenge for anyone, much less two people who must agree on it, no matter what one's age, income, or general standard of living. No sooner have you planned a good budget than a pipe starts to leak and you have to pay a big plumbing bill. Spending money sometimes just can't be helped.

The issues for couples will be the same whether they're discussing a painting that costs two hundred thousand dollars that he thinks is a waste of money but she wants, or they're talking about spending money on premium ice cream for the family. It's all about values, control, fear, childhood tapes that play in our head, and entitlement. The list goes on and on.

Maryanne's Story: Discussing Financial Stress

Maryanne was an upbeat and warm woman in her early thirties. She attended graduate school and was raising three children. Her husband of nine years, Alex, was growing increasingly overwhelmed by the changes in his work situation and their finances. Maryanne admitted that she didn't know how to deal with the issues he would bring up.

"I'd get overwhelmed," she said, "and because I

don't know anything about it all, I guess I spaced out a lot when he brought it up. He talked about things, but then I would just go watch something on TV or check my e-mail; I wouldn't really try to follow. I was brought up with nice things. I'd go to babyGap and get another little outfit and not think it was a big deal."

Alex was a devoted husband, and he and Maryanne had a date night each week. She said, "He always wanted to have a really great relationship, not a mediocre marriage. So it was always important to him to have one night each week for fun and just to check in with each other, like, how are we doing? But then for a while, Alex wanted our date night, which is always on Wednesday, to be an appointment with a marital therapist so that maybe in that context, sitting down with someone else, I could get an idea of what was going on and what he needed from me."

Maryanne was pursuing a psychology degree, but it was her husband, a more mathematical type, who saw the value in a formal meeting with a third party to discuss financial stress each week. "We went for a couple of months, and I was able to start getting it, when we all talked, about how things were going and also to understand that he needs me to listen and try to be supportive, of us and of his stresses.

"So when his firm cut our health insurance, I didn't just go 'Uh huh' like I would have before our meetings and ignore it. I knew to say, 'Tell me more about that. What does that mean for us?' When he told me it meant that one of our kids could get sick and we'd be paying for it for the rest of our lives, I was able to understand how stressed he was. Later that day, when he told me that he'd found medical plans for all of us, I was able to appreciate what that meant. I didn't have to understand the details and deductibles, or whatever, but I could be part of the situation, and he appreciated that I got it. Now I know that when I don't buy an extra something, it helps us."

Trading Life for Goods: The Spending Plan

In their classic financial book, *Your Money or Your Life: 9 Steps to Transforming Your Relationship with Money and Achieving Financial Independence,* Vicki Robin, Joe Dominguez, and Monique Tilford explain how to forget about budgets and deprivation and instead create a spending plan. A spending plan applies to the ultra wealthy and to those struggling with basics. It's something that the authors advocate whether you're twenty or past eighty.

It's established that you have to spend money. Creating a spending plan is simply about empowerment not deprivation, exercising control rather than being controlled.

We trade life for goods. Which goods, the authors ask, provide the most return? Be aware that a trade has been made, then use this awareness to make choices about what will be worth the trade to you. This helps you to formulate the spending plan. Is it worth the twenty extra hours you have to work to trade in your old espresso machine for a better one? Maybe, maybe not—it's your value system.

What We've Done Without

As difficult as it can be to get rid of some of the things we're used to having, it's helpful to remember that these things really aren't necessary for happiness. Consider this list:

Cell phone or smartphone

Laptop or desktop computer

E-mail

Internet

Facebook

Twitter

Cable television

HDTV

Tivo or DVR

Rearview camera in the car

All of these important items could not possibly be the key to happiness, unless we were never happy until about ten years ago, because these things were either not yet invented or not yet available to the general public. Of course, now that we're used to them it would be a struggle to give up or reduce our use of some of these items and services. If you are going to try to do so, make it a struggle about practicality, not the serious loss of happiness and fun. Those are available with or without these items.

Is it worth a thousand hours of work to send your child to a better college? That depends. Will he or she learn more? Only you can decide. There is no right or wrong here, just an awareness that might not have been present before.

If you're a stay-at-home parent, the work you do enables your partner to earn more money; this is a legally established principle in the case of divorce. Everyone who works—and stay-at-home mothers and fathers are some of the hardest-working people on the planet—is effectively trading his or her life energy for some version of material gain. It shows respect for that work when there's a financial plan; it means that there is a consciousness about how the money leaves the household.

Tracking Your Expenses Is to Money What Food Diaries Are to Dieting

Writing down where your money goes is the universally acknowledged way to improve everything financial. Tracking your expenses this way is what keeping a food diary is to dieting. When you first start keeping track, don't feel that you have to change anything. Just start writing. Most couples don't like to do this. They'll say it's a good idea, but there's something pathetic about running around with a frayed index card, recording the price of everything as you buy it. You don't have to do it that way. Use technology. Text your expenses to one another and save the messages, or store them in an e-mail to yourself. Just keep track.

Before you start, sit down together and make a list of the things you own that have given you the most pleasure. Look around your house. If you had to leave your home for a hurricane or a wildfire, what would you take with you? What would you replace first? What things give you the most pleasure? What did you spend money on that was a life changer? Write it down or e-mail it to yourself. This is a nice conversation to have together, and reminiscing about good things is always fun.

Now keep track for one week. At the end of the week, take a look at what you spent. Where did the money go? If you track your spending for a month, you'll really get a sense of what's going on. You'll also be able to see if the expenses in any way fall into the categories of those things that you initially agreed gave you the highest degree of satisfaction. Did the expenses fit your value system? Couples can have wide variations in their value systems. The partners may have separate goals; thus, when incomes or stock dividends go down, their choices of where to cut are going to be different. Before you can compromise, you need to know how you spend and what is truly important to you.

Two Mutually Exclusive Desires: The Ultimate Recipe for Unhappiness

An ancient Eastern saying is that "The root of unhappiness is the desire for two things that are mutually exclusive." As you analyze your lists, be aware of this truth. Do your value system and your spending habits conflict?

Dawn, twenty-five, desperately wanted to move out of her mother's apartment and be independent, but she also wanted a cell phone package that only a CEO would really need. Ultimately, these desires were mutually exclusive. If she wanted to live independently on her salary, she could only afford the essentials on a cell phone. She wouldn't accept this reality, so she kept borrowing money to buy cell phone applications.

A couple of years ago, Dawn's boyfriend and his father had convinced her to join them in buying a home with no money down. The home, it turned out, wasn't worth what they had paid for it. Dawn had lost her job recently, and she and her boyfriend had broken up over the financial pressures. Dawn's mother, Stacy, worried a lot about the situation. She was a single mother and didn't understand her daughter's disconnect from reality.

"It's like she doesn't want to deal with the reality," Stacey said. "She spends all this extra money everywhere, and now she's living with us. It's confusing to me." Dawn spent money the same way a lot of her friends did, and Stacey understood that our culture has become one of constant consumerism and that as a parent, she gave her daughter a lot more than her parents had given her.

"We gave them the idea that it's normal to buy and do unnecessary things," Stacy said. "Not to sound like an old crank, but when I was her age I was already raising her on very little money. I wasn't looking at celebrity magazines and thinking, you know, I should really go get that French manicure. I didn't start getting manicures until my thirties, when I had set up my own business and I had a meeting or something. Now the realities are changing, and she's operating on an old paradigm. It worries me."

Ben is a foreign-born, attractive man in his late fifties. A handyman in Miami Beach, he owns a lot of expensive property. In spite of his wealth, he drives a twenty-five-year-old car and grudgingly buys a new pair of jeans once a year. He's lonely and wants to settle down.

When Gary asked him about his new relationship, Ben said, "I like her very much. So nice. And I don't like to be so alone. But I don't want to stay with her because she'll make me use all my money." He laughed and shook his head.

"Wasn't it worth it, though?" Gary asked. It's good to save, but how about enjoying life with someone you love? Was the woman a gold digger? Surely she wouldn't spend all his money.

"All of it she'll spend," Ben moaned. "When she finds out I'm not poor like she thinks, she will want her supper in a nice restaurant."

Take a hard look at what you want versus what you spend money on. One man we know, a well-educated physician, complains that his wife isn't affectionate with him. One gets the impression that there isn't a lot going on for them intimacy-wise. He questions every purchase she makes. She continues to spend anyway. Although she has back pain and wanted to replace their uncomfortable mattress, he refused to agree to this purchase. If you're cheap and withholding from your spouse, and you draw the line at things that are important, you're expressing hostility through "budgeting." If you want a good life in the bedroom but won't let your partner buy a comfortable mattress, you are setting yourself up to be miserable.

Melisa: I don't think Gary has ever questioned a purchase I made for my comfort. There's an element of trust there, but there's also a spirit of generosity that has to be cultivated across the board, in all aspects of the relationship. Even if you're being aware financially, be generous in small, personal ways. Women get so much of that kind of nurturing and generosity from other women: mothers, sisters, friends. It's nice when a woman can also expect that from the man in her life. When men are generous in their attitudes, women respond in kind.

Here are some universal categories to chart in your spending plan. Ask each other and make a list of what brings you the most satisfaction in your life. Write how much you're spending in each category for a week or on a monthly basis. Carry the list with you and jot down every purchase you make.

- Housing, mortgage, or rent payments

- Home maintenance

- Food and drink: Krug champagne or a wine cooler from a bottle at the chili cook-off? Which is better? That's a personal choice. We once went to a barbecue where the host cut the chicken into weird little pieces. You had to keep going up to the grill and asking for more. He saved money, but nobody had much fun there. Food can be a charged issue for people. Combined with money, it's a powder keg. Fortunately, the Internet has many ways to address this. Just type "money saving tips" or more specific keywords into any search engine. Advice abounds. Include meals out in your budget, even if it's just a pizza or a burger.

- Electricity: If no matter what you do, your bill stays the same, check the meter yourself and make sure that the company is not estimating or averaging based on previous months when you weren't trying to save.

- Water (doesn't it come from the sky for free?)

- Gas

- Insurance in general: Insurance rates vary so widely that you need someone knowledgeable in this area to help you.

Get a referral from a friend and check rates yourself on the Internet.

- Health insurance
- Life insurance
- Auto insurance: This is where your insurance research can make a big difference. State law changes, and the savings can be in the thousands, depending on what you need to carry by law and if you lease or own your car.
- Clothing: Stick to a realistic amount of clothing by keeping track of your purchases. Clothing prices are marked up, and there are many discounts online. A popular Web site is Budget Fashionista (http://www.thebudgetfashionista.com), and fashion magazines have their own Web sites, which often list valuable offers.
- Car payments and maintenance
- Doctors: You will have to make copayments for a specialist who's partly covered by your insurance. If you have the kind of plan that covers out-of-network providers, learn about the "reasonable and customary fees" it mentions before you visit a specialist. An insurance company will say that it will pay 80 percent of these fees, but you will be shocked if you get an inflated bill because the doctor you visited has fees that are well beyond what your insurance company will cover.

    If you're a plastic surgery junkie, this category could be a major expense for you. Our friend Ceil went to a South American country a few years ago and had every conceivable plastic surgery procedure for around three dollars.

They also gave her great painkillers and a steak dinner. Consult with your doctor before going abroad to save money on surgery.

We included Ceil's story here in an attempt to be funny, but we've learned that behind every joke there's a little truth. The *New York Times* has reported that people are traveling overseas to save money on surgeries. Blue Cross Blue Shield of South Carolina, among other insurance companies, has sent American doctors to evaluate foreign hospitals. The doctors found the hospitals impressive, and now Blue Cross Blue Shield offers payment for travel expenses and as much as ten thousand dollars in cash for those who are willing to go abroad for surgeries. The article cites some of the downsides to "outsourcing" surgery, like being away from your family and your regular doctor.

- Pharmaceuticals: Some people cut their pills in half. Some experts say that this isn't a good idea, because the medicine is not always evenly dispersed within a pill. Some people skip dosages to save money or take medications that have been prescribed for others. These things can be dangerous. Ask your doctor for advice and to write prescriptions when appropriate for the less costly generic brands.

- Veterinarian care: Our household now includes two small dogs and a golden retriever, a rescued one-eyed Persian cat and her nonpedigreed cat friend (both of whom think they're dogs), a dwarf hamster, a parrot that can't fly, two companion finches, and an outdoor turtle.

We could easily spend a fortune on veterinarian care. We don't buy fancy dog strollers and doggie playpens as the couple we noticed on the beach the other day seems to do; still the animal upkeep certainly adds up. We notice the staff at the vet's office greets us very enthusiastically when we arrive.

In addition to all the various pet foods, there are visits to the veterinarian for checkups, shots, procedures, and treatments, which vary tremendously in cost. It definitely pays to look around. In Manhattan, a dog dental procedure can cost a thousand dollars, while the same procedure costs a fraction of that one county away. Our veterinarian recently included a free teeth cleaning as part of a surgery that our dog had to have. We went over every charge before the surgery so that we wouldn't be surprised with extra costs.

- Telephones: Phone bills these days can equal the gross national product of a small country. This item just screams for investigation and awareness. There are combination home phone, Internet, and cable television services. Some people have chosen to give up their landlines. Programs like Skype allow you to talk and see a loved one across the globe or one state away for free (you need an Internet connection, a computer, and a webcam—many newer computer models have a webcam built in). Oprah uses Skype to bring people on the show from everywhere. We enjoy talking with people we've never met through Skype. Check and recheck your cell phone plans, which are always changing to stay competitive. Research can bring you big savings.
- Gifts
- Charities

- Beauty and grooming
- Tuition
- Day care and babysitting
- Extracurricular activities
- Tutoring or lessons
- Family vacations
- Summer camp
- Newspapers and periodicals
- Home repair or renovations
- Gym memberships or trainers
- Electronics (computers and television upkeep or purchase)
- Cleaning help or housekeeper
- Therapies and treatments
- Financial gifts to children or grandchildren
- Work expenses: gifts for the boss or an assistant

Other items that are unique to your lifestyle and situation might not be listed here. If they are not, list them yourself. Find out what your life costs and see how you want to spend, how you want to trade your life energy and your time with your loved ones for the items you have purchased. Remember, it's about empowerment and taking control, not losing it.

8

The One-Week Relationship Program That Will Change Your Life

A pattern of creating distance because of financial difficulties can be very hard to break out of in a relationship. The sooner you can bridge the gap between you, the better for the relationship. Recognizing how complicated it can be to come together about your finances, we wanted to offer a clear, quick plan to help you move your relationship into a new, healthier place.

This plan does not assume ongoing major relationship issues and resentments that have remained unspoken for years. If one or both of you have cheated multiple times and you haven't resolved the issues around that, you need more than this one-week plan. However, if you love each other and your relationship is basically sound, but you just find that you have locked horns about money, have become angry and resentful, have found it easier to shut down than say you're scared, or have felt distant from each other, then here is some clear help to correct your issues in one week.

The reason the tension can take over so quickly is that you've allowed life to make a wedge in your love. To break out of this situation, you have to get back to your love and take control of your life as much as you can. Love is a wonderful thing, and just a little focus on it develops a hope that instantly strengthens us.

Every day of this week, ramp up the music. Music is a good thing. It can be meaningful and spiritual, and it tells everyone around that life is happening and that you're not waiting for something to happen in order to move forward and sing a song. There is something about music that takes you over and can improve the mood in your relationship. It's freeing and can help you to focus on being close with each other. Play whatever music is appealing to either or both of you in the main common rooms of your home.

Sunday: The Conversation

Although we've begun the plan on a Sunday, you can tailor it to start on any day of the week. The first and most important goal is to get the two of you talking meaningfully again. Messages of understanding, love, and apology may be needed. Hope and commitment to teamwork are vital. Remember these important points to set up a successful discussion:

- Have the conversation when there will be no interruptions. Cell phones, e-mail devices, television, and radio must all be turned off. Your children may not intrude, so they should be out, involved in an activity, or sleeping. Agree not to answer the home phone if it rings.

- The conversation is to take no more than ten minutes. Whenever serious issues are brought up, there's a likelihood that the conversation will deteriorate into arguing and blaming. Many people say they wished they would've just stopped a discussion when the points were made and agreed on. That's intense enough, for a start, and then you need a break. You can always return to discuss any issue at a later time. Don't risk undoing the conversation; it's crucial to turning things around and making your relationship different.

- Have the conversation only when you're well fed and rested. As the Hulk says, "You don't want to see me when I'm angry." You don't want to see each other when you're famished or tired. Nothing good usually comes out of midnight conversations, when at least one person is exhausted, or right before dinner, when you're hungry.

- Touch your spouse. Hold your spouse's hand, if possible, for a moment.

Remember, this is not the time to launch into a detailed talk about money or the details of what you're going to do as a couple. It's only to set the record straight, agree to turn things around, and start the one-week plan. After that, end the conversation with the understanding that you can make time for conversations about the stressful stuff.

Once you've found the time to sit down, include the topics listed on pages 124 to 127 on your agenda. In each case, we have provided suggested wording to give you an idea of how to begin your discussion. The text following the asterisks represents something you will probably want to say. (It may go first or last, depending on the topic being discussed.) Then choose one of the non-asterisked choices from the list, if it applies to your situation. (Note that topics 6 and 7 are made up of asterisked lines only.) If any piece of the conversation doesn't fit for you, come up with your own caring comments.

Topic 1. Highlight the importance of the relationship

* Honey, I want to take just a few minutes to tell you something. Please don't respond until I'm finished. It won't take more than a couple of minutes. This is really important to me and hopefully to us. I love you.

   I know that: (Choose one.)

   ___ we've been doing okay lately.

   ___ we've been out of sorts.

   ___ things have been bad with us lately.

* But our relationship is too important to me (and the kids), and hopefully to you, for us not to get back to a good place with each other as soon as possible.

Topic 2. Acknowledge the difficult place you're in

* I know that: (Choose one.)

   ___ we've hit a rough spot.

   ___ things have been really tough.

   ___ things have been kind of miserable.

   ___ we've been lost from each other.

Topic 3. Take the blame away

> (Choose one.)

> ___ I don't want to blame anymore. I'm done with that and am genuinely sorry for hurting your feelings.

> ___ I don't want to be blamed anymore and I'm genuinely sorry for what I did.

> ___ Can we please be done with the blaming? I'm genuinely sorry for hurting you and for my part in what's happened.

* I just want us to be able to move forward and start talking calmly about solutions to this instead of:

> (Choose one.)

> ___ arguing over everything.

> ___ shouting at each other about events in the past.

> ___ staying away from each other and not knowing what to say.

Topic 4. Express the desire to work together on the problems

> (Choose one or more.)

> ___ I want to get back to things as they were.

> ___ I want to get back to being loving to each other.

* I want to work through this together and really be there for each other.

* I know we can do it and I'm willing to put my all into it.

Topic 5. Focus on creatively achieving your goals

* Let's stop wasting our energy on what's gone wrong and put our time into making things right from now on. Let's build ourselves up and give each other strength. Look what our love has done so far:

    (Choose one or more.)

    ___ It's given us beautiful children.

    ___ It's given us so much happiness in the past.

    ___ It's given us this beautiful home full of love.

    ___ It's given us close friends and a community.

Topic 6. Commitment to frequent, positive talking

* I want us to get back to being happy about life. I want to focus on being in love.

* Let's make time to talk about the things we need to discuss and do it in a calm manner, as a team, the way we always hoped it would be.

Topic 7. Commitment to the one-week plan

* I want to show you something I've been reading. It is a simple one-week plan to help us regain our focus and quickly improve our life together.

* It includes ways to talk about our financial situation and to create time for ourselves (and ways we can talk to the children about our financial situation).

* Please, for us (and the kids), let's commit to this for just one week and see where we are after that.

Topic 8. Reassurance, hope, love

* I know we can get through this. We can be really good at this together. I love you, and that alone makes me hopeful. We have to be able to do this.

   (Choose one.)

   ___ I don't want to lose us.

   ___ I don't want to lose you.

   ___ I don't want to lose the best part of us.

   ___ I need your help.

   ___ I want to feel in love with you and work together.

Monday: Date Night

This one-week plan calls for three date nights, which is much more than some couples can manage. The premise is important, however: change happens more quickly for a couple when the individuals are reminded how much they can enjoy their time together. A couple will often come to Gary, asking him to help the two of them stop fighting. He explains that he can typically do that within a session or two, but they still won't be happy. Happiness is not the absence of sadness. It comes from proactive attention to spending pleasant time together.

For this week, therefore, do everything you can to have the date nights. If you can't find, afford, or trust a babysitter, then at least plan to do something fun or interesting after the kids are in bed and asleep. Don't just watch television. Read to each other;

play cards, backgammon, or a board game; or surf funny things online together. The best idea is still to go out, even if you spend no more than a few dollars on a pot of hot tea.

Date Night: Just for the Two of You. Have Fun

In every book Gary has written for couples, he has outlined what the date night is all about. Getting back to having fun with each other is so crucial to any change for a couple that it's worth discussing some of the main obstacles to creating meaningful time together. What causes us to fall in love and decide to get married is often the very thing we tend to drop or omit once we are married or committed to each other. We dated, had fun, talked about politics and philosophy, and giggled a lot. After "settling down," however, it's easy to stop knowing the light side of each other, and sometimes we don't even know what to do to have fun together anymore.

Dating was once a great part of our relationship with our partners, so why not get back to it? It's a simple investment that pays immediate dividends. Make this a time that is just for the two of you. Don't have another couple or your depressed brother tagging along. There's time for them later. Let's face it, when couples go out together, the men and the women usually pair off in separate conversations. It can be great fun, but it is not time that you and your spouse are spending growing together as a couple. Friends can meet you after the first two hours on that night, if you like. However, don't plan to go out to dinner with friends and then think you'll spend your two hours alone at the end of the evening. It never happens.

Men tend to assume that anything but work falls under the domain of "My wife will take care of it." Don't make this true of the date night or your marriage. As a couple, review the newspaper to find the best happenings around town. Planning your date night together in and of itself creates a more loving atmosphere. Consider what you'd like to do with your time together that would be of interest to both of you.

Do your best to go out somewhere with each other, but have a plan so that you don't just get in the car and then wonder what to do next. That's never a positive moment. That says that nobody here has been concerned enough to plan anything.

Avoid the dinner-and-a-movie thing as much as possible. It can be quite expensive, a movie is not interactive, and dinner can be too interactive. The pressure to make fascinating conversation after being out of sorts can make you fail miserably.

Date-Night Restrictions

There is one simple rule for the date night: avoid talking about money, work, or your kids. You might wonder what you will talk about, because that's all you ever talk about. However, we can confidently say that when you were dating and falling in love you were not talking incessantly about the stresses of money, work, and kids. If you had been, we are sure that you would never have gotten hitched in the first place. Don't worry, we've created other times for you to discuss these subjects.

Every couple needs some private space in which to develop a "couple personality" that can handle life stressors in stride. Remember when you had a song that was just for the two of you? Was the song called "Kids and Mortgage Payments and My Damn Boss?"

We didn't think so. Your special song was about love and a focus on two people seeing something wonderful in each other that no one else took the time to see. Take the time to notice this and get back to being a unit—and find a new song, already! Be young and in love for at least a couple of hours on your date night. Soon you'll be singing a new song and feeling rejuvenated even when you're not on a date.

Creating a Private Place for Your Relationship

In addition to having a date night, every couple needs space in their own home to just be together. This week of change involves bold moves to show each other that you are no longer going to be entangled in the problems you're having; instead, you're going to put some energy into focusing on the love between the two of you. If you just talk about it but don't do anything to help it happen, the plan will fail before it begins.

If you have children, your greatest challenge to uninterrupted time with your spouse might be managing your children's nighttime routine. Let's face it, by the time we're done dealing with the kids each day, we are often in no shape to spend quality time with each other. How many of us have a calm, quiet home at night in which all the children are tucked into bed and sleeping, leaving a delicious, cozy hour for us to connect? It gets worse as the children get older, because they might go to sleep later than you do. There is no calm and quiet if adolescents are lurking around every corner with food, music, and text message conversations going on with four people.

It is simply too easy to feel hopeless and lose this battle. You might be years into your marriage, and it may seem impossible to change your household circumstances, but this is not true. You don't need an entire house to connect with your spouse. You just need some closed space, and you can usually find it in your bedroom.

Most couples tend to treat the bedroom as an extension of the playroom. Life comes at us at a quick pace, and having your child bring his shoe to your bedroom so you can help him put it on while you finish getting dressed seems like a good multitasking system. When your child needs to use the bathroom really badly, and hers is taken or she's right near yours, what's the difference? When you all want to snuggle up as a family and watch TV together, what better place than the marital bed? Children generally envision a revolving door to their parents' bedroom, where Mom and Dad are easily accessible for everything from homework help to serious life discussions. In part, our worry that our children will not feel close to us or won't share necessary thoughts and feelings with us has fueled this around-the-clock attention and access.

Gary has spent a large part of his life trying to help parents to truly understand their children. This ability takes a great deal of effort and focus as well as skilled communication.

As a father of five, Gary has experienced large doses of parental guilt, worrisome thoughts that a child is suffering alone, not finding the right time to be able to connect with him. However, this worry about the importance of being there for our kids must not be allowed to creep its way into debilitating our spousal time and relationship.

Those of us who are couples with children usually have

no space of our own. We have to travel to hotels without our children just to find an untouched space that we can call our own. It is simply unhealthy to feel that there is no space for the relationship in our own home. How many times have you been in your bathroom having a conversation with your child on the other side of the door while your spouse is somewhere in the bedroom? There is something wrong with this scenario, and even if it has become the natural cadence and rhythm in your home, don't give up on creating a different rhythm. It's a good idea to consider changes in the way you manage your bedroom. Your marriage needs a private place, a sense of seclusion, so that both of you can express the private part of your marital personalities.

Here are some suggestions for achieving that:

1. *Limit your children's access to your bedroom.* There are usually quite a few other rooms in your home. We're not suggesting that there be some fanatical restrictions—just a healthy respect for your privacy. It may not always work (it often didn't in our house), but you have to try.

2. *Use other rooms for what they were intended.* You have a kitchen, a place to eat as a family, and a living room or a family room, where you can all watch TV, read, or surf the Internet. Keep those activities in their designated places. Don't let your kids bring food into your bedroom to snack on while watching television together. Watch television or do other family activities in the room that is the intended space for that. We're not much for families watching lots of television together, but we use it as an example, knowing that many families do. If the family

computer is in your bedroom, move it out. If you're worried about the kids getting online without you knowing about it, learn how to place a password on the computer so that your children can't even start it up without your knowledge.

3. *Lock your bedroom door.* When you need privacy after the activities of the day are over, sequester yourselves by closing and locking the door. It doesn't imply that you are locking your child out. It says only that you and your spouse want and deserve some private, uninterrupted time. It doesn't have to imply to your children that you're having sex, especially if you begin to lock your door regularly. If your child needs access in the middle of the night, a simple tap on the door can let you know. When the door is locked, partners act differently, knowing that a child cannot easily interrupt. When a couple has a sense of being absolutely alone, it offers an aura of calm that says, "We can talk about stuff now, because the demands of life are out *there* and can't easily get to us."

4. *Keep your children out of your bathroom as much as possible.* We know that it sometimes seems easier to have a child just use your bathroom, but avoid it as much as you can, for it quickly leads to the kids having common access to your bedroom. It also detracts from the intimacy of your bedroom. Enough said.

5. *Keep work out of the bed.* Once you're alone in your bedroom, don't invite other intense pieces of life into it. Shuffling work papers and tapping incessantly on the laptop or the BlackBerry are all an invasion of the privacy of

the marital space. Try to avoid or change the idea that your bed is the proper place for things that create stress and detract from your intimacy. Bonus points if you can keep work out of your bedroom completely. Some couples don't have a separate home office or even a space in the kitchen in which to manage the business of the home, so they are forced to use the bedroom. Still, do your best to find some small workplace outside your bedroom, even if you have to deal with bills at the kitchen table once a week or at your workplace. Do whatever you can to move the stressors of life out of your bedroom so that you have a space for both of you to focus only on each other and your loving intimacy.

Finding Time after the Children Are Asleep

The first thing you might need to do to allow for uninterrupted time together is to create changes in your children's nighttime routine. Our children present us with a complicated dilemma. We love them as much as, if not more than, life itself, and our lives are wrapped up in caring for them. This, in part, causes us to allow their needs and their desires to grab our attention. Children draw so much strength and love from their parents that they seek constant attention from us. It's just too easy to become consumed by our children's lives and allow our marriages to suffer. Most couples see "marital time" as whatever time is left over after dealing with the kids. Usually, it seems to be less than zero; by the time we look at each other at the end of the evening, we can barely speak.

It is crucial to our children that they have parents who are happy together. This particular fact gives you permission to find time with your spouse *even if it comes at the expense of time with your child* (keeping in mind that the amount of time with your spouse has been relatively little). At some point, you will recognize that you'll never have "enough" time with your children. They are always going to crave more time and attention, until the teenage years, so the only way you will ever have time with your spouse is to make it happen and to teach your children to respect that time.

Imagine the difference between children who grow up in a home with parents who love each other and show it and children who don't. Watch your youngest child's face the next time you and your spouse are kissing, embracing, or dancing together in the kitchen. Children's eyes light up at such scenes. The loving time you spend with your spouse will not detract from your children's lives. They will feel at peace in their home and will be more likely to grow into secure individuals who will choose to love wisely and keep the romance alive. You will also significantly increase your own ability to be happy and calmer around your children, because you are in a happier marital space. Here are two main areas to consider:

- *The key to sleeping children is tired children.* By the time young children hit the sack, they are not as tired as you think they are. As much as they've worked all day in school and had physical education classes or sports activities, children have an abundance of energy. They sometimes amaze their parents on a weekend, when they are playing a sport for hours in the hot sun and then spend two hours in a swimming pool. Keep in mind that if your

135

child is not going to sleep easily at night, the first thing to consider is if he or she is getting enough physical activity to be able to go to sleep on time. You may need to adjust your child's schedule to include significantly more outdoor playtime after school.

- *Teach your kids that the evening is over.* As your children grow older, they're not going to be asleep by eight-thirty at night. They might be up until long after you're tucked away. This doesn't mean that you have to be at their beck and call for the entire evening, however. Children can be taught that at a certain time (let's say nine-thirty) Mom and Dad will be in their room with the door closed, spending uninterrupted marital time. You will need to enforce this for only a short while before they really get it and respect it. There should not be a knock on your door unless it is some sort of emergency or the child is not feeling well. Consider instituting a nine o'clock deadline for any requests for the next day: if your kids need money or something signed or reviewed, it will not happen after nine o'clock, which means that if they forget to do it before then, they'll have to just make do the next day. To avoid hectic morning routines, don't consider doing it the next morning, either. This is easier said than done, we know, but there will be an increase in the amount of time that you and your spouse have together.

We are not suggesting that you separate from the children. These are just the simplest ideas for creating a home atmosphere that's conducive to a happy, loving marriage. This will translate to a very happy home for everyone who lives there.

Making Love: Bedroom Time

You may not feel ready for the bedroom yet. After all, it was just yesterday that you made your move to break the ice with each other in the first place. Before you get to the work of the money issues, you have to remind each other that you were and are a couple and want to feel like one.

Sometimes the body sends signals to the brain about feeling better. If you're depressed, consider taking a walk. Friends will sometimes coax a depressed person to start walking daily for exercise, to get the endorphins going and send the mind the message that the body is moving forward and getting better.

Being together physically as a couple tells our minds and our bodies that we're on the mend, that we're moving forward with intimacy, and that we're not waiting indefinitely to start living as a couple again. If you aren't ready for physical expression, set aside this time to educate yourselves, discuss new ideas, and share the things that appeal to you.

It is crucial that this time be about romance and love, kind words, and thoughtful gestures, in and out of the bedroom. A loving text message or phone call and a thoughtful, inexpensive gift—a magazine, a single flower, a favorite food—show that you were thinking of your love. In his book *The Truth about Cheating*, Gary discusses simple, essential information and techniques to ensure that your lovemaking is mutually pleasing and that it draws you closer. You can also visit his Web site (http://www.mgaryneuman.com), where he discusses many of those techniques and some new ideas. Because he hears from so many people about this, he has included many of their questions and comments on the site.

Tuesday: The Financial Discussion and a Family Dinner

In the previous chapter, we outlined a plan for discussing your financial concerns and suggested that the discussion be limited to thirty minutes, a rule you must enforce from the start. Now is the time not to blame but rather to deal with the reality. You may need a great deal of clarification: ask each other exactly what is your debt, what is your income versus your expenses, and what is your expected upcoming income or debt. It's also time to discuss what you can do immediately to deal with any part of the problem as well as any ideas for trying to solve the whole problem. Brainstorm about how to find ideas and other people you might want to talk to, such as those who are in similar situations and might have helpful information. Then make a list of all the things you came up with.

End the conversation with a positive, reassuring statement, like "I know it's a little tough to handle, but I feel so much better knowing that we're working on this as a team. Let's do whatever it takes to be there for each other through this time."

Also on Tuesday, establish a time for tonight and the next three nights when everyone in your family can sit down for a relaxing dinner. Eating together gives the people who live together a greater sense of family. Family dinners have become a thing of the past in so many homes. Life is so busy, children of different ages are doing many different activities, and working parents are keeping fluctuating schedules. Believe us, it's worth putting your effort into this one. Many parents forgo the dinner because they picture a complicated meal with everyone sitting quietly for an hour, but that doesn't have to be the case at all.

Depending on the ages and the schedules of your family members, regular family dinners may not work for now. It doesn't matter; sit down with whoever can be there. The idea of cutting vegetables while talking to your children is wonderful, but it's not essential for enjoying the benefits of the family dinner. Whether you're serving a frozen dinner, a pizza, or a home-cooked meal, just sitting together for even twenty minutes gives everyone the message that "we're a family and moving through life together." Forget high expectations. Just eating together, reviewing the day, and laughing for a moment—any pleasant conversation at all—sends the message that you belong together and want to touch base no matter how far apart you have wandered the rest of our day.

Consider these very real benefits of the family dinner:

- Teens who ate regular frequent family dinners were 40 percent more likely to get As and Bs in school than teenagers whose families ate separately, according to research provided by Columbia University.

- A survey of a thousand teens by the National Center on Addiction and Substance Abuse at Columbia University found that nearly half of them thought that dinnertime was the best time to talk to their parents about something important. More than 80 percent of the teens said that they preferred having dinner with their families to eating alone.

- A University of Minnesota study found that teens who had family dinners five or more times a week were 42 percent less likely to drink alcohol, 59 percent less likely to smoke cigarettes, and 66 percent less likely to try marijuana.

Promoting a healthier diet, discouraging eating disorders, and improving your children's vocabulary are three additional benefits of the family dinner that show how powerful it is in creating a stronger family. Don't eliminate it from this week's plan because you don't think you'll be able to keep it up. You don't have to have it five times a week for it to be successful for your family. Even if after this week you have the family dinner just two times a week, it will be beneficial to all of you. But for this week especially, use it to focus on and send a message of unity and togetherness, even as your family is experiencing other changes. Dinner together says that "one thing here is not going to change: our loving focus on one another."

Wednesday: A Mini-Date and a Family Dinner

Tonight's mini-date doesn't have to take place outside the home, although that's ideal. It does have to last for at least one hour, however. Follow the rules for date night about restricting conversations about money, work, and kids. The purpose is to create some space to get back to enjoying each other after you've had the money talk the night before. Tonight says that no matter how complicated the circumstances, you are back together and will keep drawing on the love in your relationship, no matter what.

On the second family dinner night, go around the table and let each person say one nice thing about each child at the table. It can be a compliment or a simple appreciative comment.

Thursday: A Talk with Your Kids, a Mini–Money Discussion, and Another Family Dinner

Refer to chapter 9 on talking about money with your kids, and have that conversation with your children.

Afterward, have another open discussion as a couple as a continuation of the discussion from Tuesday. This one can revisit some of the issues. Don't reopen the problems; rather, discuss any further thoughts on the ideas. Perhaps you had decided at that meeting that each of you was going to check on something and now you're ready to report on it: the exact amount owed on a credit card bill, when your lease is up, a court date hearing, the name of an attorney that a friend used, or information on jobs from a friend. Decide which ideas to continue to explore and perhaps add some new ones you have thought of since. Set a twenty-minute time limit on this meeting.

Friday: A Family Night Followed by Couple Time

We waited until Friday night, not a school night, to allow for some free time for your kids. It's also the day after you discussed money issues with them. Tonight will remind everyone what your family is all about. You've already shown that your family can deal directly with the problems; now show your kids that the family is committed to love no matter what the circumstances.

Remember that children mostly want their parents' attention and time. You don't have to go out and spend lots of money. Your time with your kids can be spent visiting a park, playing sports, or doing any activity that your kids enjoy. It can be having a family dinner for which everyone cooks together and then playing a board game for an hour or so after. Children love time with the whole family focused on having fun. It sends a powerful, positive message that your children will draw on for the rest of their lives.

When you see yourselves loving your kids and them loving you back, you will realize that creating a family is one of the most amazing things you've done as a couple. Give yourselves a moment of congratulations for that.

Later, make love. You give to others all day long in raising your children, and now the two of you deserve some personal pleasure and the feeling of giving and being given to in the most intimate way. This is for both of you.

If you do not have kids, or they are grown up and not at home, this night is a reminder of the love that you as a couple are drawing upon. You've had the money talks; now you need to show each other that your energy will remain focused on love. Love, not struggle, will define this relationship.

Saturday: Date Night

You've come a long way: you're recommitting to your relationship; you're dealing with your issues up front in a progressive, solution-oriented manner; you're involving your kids in your financial issues in a healthy way; you're having fun and making love. Tonight is another opportunity for exploration by the two of you of how powerful you feel when you allow yourselves to shut off the world and be alone with each other. Since it's a Saturday, try to grab more than two hours to be out or alone in your bedroom to enjoy each other. Soon you will remember why you became involved with each other in the first place. You may choose to engage in physical intimacy, but only if it flows comfortably from the evening for you.

By Sunday morning, you might be surprised at how much things have turned around. As you move forward, don't let what got you this far fall by the wayside. Commit to a weekly money discussion, a weekly date night, lovemaking at least once or twice a week, and a weekly family-focused evening of play with your kids. Sometimes, make the family night about giving—for example, visit a home for the aged or help to feed people at a homeless shelter or a soup kitchen. Giving makes us feel great and will give your family a sense of life's deeper meaning.

PART THREE

Bring It Home

9

What You Can Do
for Your Children

One of the most unfortunate by-products of any life struggle is its direct effect on children. So much of what we do as parents is for the purpose of providing our children a relatively happy childhood as well as a secure foundation for their adult lives. We put tons of effort into working so we can make enough money to give our children everything that we dream of giving them. We want them to have it all: nutrition, a comfortable home, a good education, clothing, proper health care, vacations, camp experiences, money set aside to help them as adults, and so on.

The subject of financial pressures can be so uncomfortable and destabilizing that many parents will simply not discuss it openly with their children. "After all, what should I say?" one woman wrote to me. "Tough luck, kid, the economy's bad." It may feel easier to avoid the subject altogether and hope for the best, but don't think that your children don't know what's going on. They see the financial pressures in everything you do and in the conversations that surround them.

It is sad but true that most kids learn about money from the arguments that their parents have within earshot. When small children hear Dad say loudly, "You're spending all of our money," they think in very concrete terms: "Oh my gosh, Mom is spending *all* of our money." Then they hear Mom say, "Do you see me buying diamonds? All I'm spending on is food and things for our children." Imagine where a kid's mind goes from there.

Lack of Information Fuels Overactive Imaginations

Children are creative beings who have wonderful imaginations. When they are not given information, they will make it up. Gary remembers being told as a kid by his mother that he shouldn't stick his arm out of the car window while they were driving. He used to love the feeling of the wind pressing against his cupped hand. He was convinced that just like in *The Flintstones*, when a huge brontosaurus steak caused the car to turn on its side, his arm would also shift the car weight and cause it to flip onto its side.

Crazy thoughts go through children's minds until an adult sets the children straight. Talking about money is kind of like the parental sex talk—so uncomfortable. We're not sure what to say, so let's hope that someone else takes care of that one. There isn't much in the way of financial education at schools yet, so children are often left to struggle through a money issue alone if you don't discuss it with them.

As a therapist, Gary has seen parents make many mistakes when communicating with their children. The biggest mistake is the idea some parents have that they must have all the answers. Parents often see themselves as a sort of encyclopedia. It seems dangerous to many parents not to have the right answer. A child might lose complete respect for the parent who doesn't know it all or, worse yet, the child might make up his or her own mind about a given topic. Parents sometimes think that if they don't have the answers, the only recourse they have is to avoid, avoid, and avoid.

It goes something like this: If your child has questions about sex and you don't know the right way to explain it, avoid it. Drugs are bad, but if your child asks if you've ever tried any, avoid answering. Changes about money are very confusing even when the market isn't crazy. If adults can't figure out how things are working, what must children think? What about the inconsistencies? What does it mean that you can't afford another pair of sneakers for your child but you just got a new car? Why doesn't Mom get a job like Trevor's mom did?

The lack of parental conversation is deafening. It screams how much a parent is missing. The most important functions of a parent are to provide stability, to offer a place to talk, and to be there while a child figures out how the world works.

Remember what was meaningful to you when you were a child. Do you remember the moments with your parents when

The Three Best Ways to Communicate with Your Kids

1. Talk to your children about your situation in an honest yet reassuring way. Describe the potential changes that all of you might experience, but give the message that the strength of your family will allow you to continue living your lives filled with love, regardless of the upcoming economic changes. Letting them know that you're in charge and that you're thinking this through puts them at ease.

2. Listen to what they have to say, and avoid quickly rescuing them with comforting words before they've had a chance to be understood by you. You can always end the conversation with a reassuring thought.

3. Be your best self and serve as a good role model during this time. When children see you calm, dealing with the situation and believing in your ability to navigate the current crisis, it reassures them. Dr. Malka Zacharowitz, a neuropsychologist, evaluates children for learning disabilities and other issues. She remarked recently on the number of children who look so sick when they come to see her. They look tense and ill, and they often act out, leading the parents to presume that there is a hyperactivity disorder.

   "They're distracted and impulsive," says Dr. Zacharowitz, "but it's because they're worried and affected by what's happening in the home. These aren't kids who are losing their homes but rather kids whose families have had to change their lifestyles. When their parents are too stressed to discuss what's going on, they don't calm the kids or model resilience. If the parents would just talk with them and model calm reassurance, I believe the children would be physically healthier."

you learned specific information? How misty-eyed do you get thinking about the time that Mom helped you with your fractions homework? What mattered was the love you received from your parents. It could have been the hugs and the cuddling, the fun road trip, or the times they reminded you how wonderful you really are.

It was never their IQ that calmed you; it was all about the love they offered. It was their love that gave you the space to develop your own style of loving—and if they were cold or unloving, no amount of intellectual acumen made up for that lack of warmth. As a parent you do not have to have the answers. Your children do not need you to solve their problems. They need you to offer love so that they can face their struggles with confidence and support.

Naturally, your children need reassurance. There is a misconception that we have to know the outcome of a situation before addressing it, but that's not really accurate. We reassure children all the time without truly knowing the future. If you've got the flu, and your five-year-old looks worried, you tell him or her that you'll be fine. It's likely that you'll get better, so you have no problem saying you'll be fine. You don't feel the need to explain to your child that there is a chance you could die from the flu, as thousands of people do every year. If you seem calm, that's good enough for a child, who will feed off your energy. Whatever comes out of your mouth is less important than the feeling you transmit.

As a parent, you need to find whatever helps you to hold it all together for the sake of not freaking out your children. When you're on a plane and there's heavy turbulence and your child looks nervously at you and asks if everything is okay, you respond with that false parental knowledge of cloud structure and descent. "Yes, everything is fine," you say. "There's bumpiness when a plane descends through the different pockets of air in the clouds." Meanwhile, what you're really thinking is "Is the pilot drunk? I'm going to vomit. Please don't let those oxygen bags drop, or else I will lose it."

Sometimes we don't have the luxury of falling apart. We keep moving through the days, holding everything in place for our children's sake. When money problems hit, they test our ability to hold everything in place, because our children will see the real changes that are happening. They cannot be hidden the way other personal issues can.

Take Care of Yourself

The pressures on parents today are many. Sometimes we just can't imagine one more thing that we "should" be doing. Simplifying life in the bad times can help us to be better parents just by giving us more quiet time.

Melisa: The mothers I've seen who have quiet time say no to committees and other causes when they need to be calmer. They turn the lights down and quiet the house before bedtime; they sit with a book or a magazine while their kids are going to sleep and ignore the phone. They brush off the guilt and the criticism and take things less personally.

When I was a young mother in my twenties, I took everything to heart. I wanted so badly to do a good job, and it devastated me when someone implied that I wasn't doing the best thing for my kids or that I was shortchanging them in some way. I thought these people must be right. My perspective finally shifted on an airplane ride home from a family wedding. The infant twins were crying, and they wouldn't stop. The other three kids were behaving pretty well, but no matter what we did, we couldn't calm the babies. We were the family from hell that you can't believe you're stuck on an airplane with for hours.

I knew from experience that they'd calm down soon, and I nicely said that to a man who started yelling at me. He didn't understand, he said, what would possess us to bring all these kids on an airplane. I started to explain about the wedding, but he cut me off, asking me what kind of mother I was and why didn't I feed those kids—anyone could see they were hungry. Didn't I have any food for them? I was shocked at his attack.

My insecurity about mothering was suddenly displaced by outrage. All of a sudden the absurdity of his attack hit me. I slapped my head with my palm and asked Gary why we hadn't thought of that: feed the babies! I congratulated the man on his brilliance and acumen. I told him it hadn't occurred to us that children require food; all the bottles and pacifiers we were coaxing them with were just props. Why, he was a genius! When was his parenting book coming out, I asked. Was he doing any lectures? Thanks, I told him, for his kindness. Could he direct me to the lobby of the plane so that I could take my children there, since they were disturbing him? Oh wait, planes don't have lobbies.

· · ·

Try not to take the things people say so personally. Many people like to make us feel bad when we can't meet our children's needs. When we take time for ourselves and make ourselves feel better about things, we have more to give to our children. Like the man on the plane, most of the people who criticize us have no idea what they're talking about. We need to be kind to ourselves, to do the things that calm us and build us up, especially when things are rough.

Stop feeling the pressure of having to be the all-knowing parent. Your child does not need to know what you'll be making when the recession is over. *Your child needs to know that your family will stay emotionally connected and that you can work together as a family on a plan to make that happen, no matter what the financial future holds for you.*

Tricia's Story: The Importance of Ballet

I was eight years old and the star of my ballet class, and I absolutely loved being there. There was talk of my being a star when I grew up, and I twirled constantly in front of my mirror, dreaming of that day. In retrospect, I'm not sure how good I was. I was in Manhattan, and there were a lot of girls in ballet.

I'll never forget coming home from school one day and seeing all my things packed up. There was a moving van outside, and my mother told me we were taking a road trip to Grandma's house for the summer. Since I had a test the next day and three weeks left in the school year, I was quite curious about this explanation. I was happy to skip school, but I wanted to know when we would go to ballet. My mother put her arm around me and told me what I guess she thought was the thing to say: she sadly explained that the ballet school had closed.

We moved to a tiny town where most people couldn't even spell "ballet," much less have any appreciation for it. It became clear that we weren't going back. Dad filtered in and out. Grandmother hated him, and the feeling seemed mutual. We stayed there for a year before moving into a little home, where we remained until I was thirteen. I later learned that my father had lost his job. I'm not sure, but somewhere in my head I have the thought that he stole some money and was fired, but I can't remember where that came from. My parents divorced then, and I knew less and less about my dad as time went on.

Today, I am a patron of the New York City Ballet. My two daughters are ballet dancers. The older one has had enough and will stop at the end of the year, but the younger one loves it and will continue. I'm thrilled. My mother passed away three years ago, and I was quite sad. When I cried at her funeral, it wasn't really because I would miss her. I was, I think, grieving for the lost opportunities, for what I never had the chance to have with her. I was sad that as much as she tried to care for me, we couldn't talk, and I never really knew who she was. She never really knew who I was, either. It still makes me cry.

The Number One Mistake Parents Make: Not Talking to Your Children

Kids are far brighter and more aware than we give them credit for being. They know something's up. When you don't talk to them, their anxiety level skyrockets; worst of all, they tend to personalize the problems in the family. They may think that school, their books, their clothes, or their favorite foods are costing too much and are the reason for the financial distress. Many children have told Gary that they have no idea what they've done to cause the problems, but it must be really bad, because their parents can't even seem to broach it with them.

We'll show you how to have conversations with your children. Be committed to talking with them every step of the way, even if you are unsure of the direction of your financial future.

Your children need you to connect with them and prove to them on a daily basis that they are worthy and deserve love. Don't be silenced by discomfort, not knowing what to say, or worrying about whether your children will ask something. You might not have the answer, but you'll have what your children need much more: the feeling that you really understand them and that together, this family can pull through anything with a lot of love and kindness.

Here is your chance to teach your child the most wonderful message about family: we survive on love, not money. Many children get the message that they have a wonderful life because of the money their parents earn; it offers them fun opportunities and lots and lots of stuff. We know, however, and it's our job to help them know, that stuff does not equal happiness.

Wealth and fame do not result in happiness. Think about how many celebrities are divorced or are estranged from their children. Economic downturns provide the chance to teach your children that love is what makes the family happy and successful.

When your children become adults, they're going to look back on these tough economic times and say, "That was when our family fell apart" or "That was when I learned how to be strong and stay close. My parents taught me how to face things and get through them." They will carry these messages with them for the rest of their lives. They will draw strength from this time. They will have less fear in life, knowing that money can come and go, that good times and bad times may come and go, but we

Messages to Send to Your Children in Times of Struggle

1. We continue to focus on love.
2. We work together as a team for one another.
3. You are a crucial part of our team.
4. Money comes and goes, but the love we focus on lasts forever.
5. We are resilient; we find ways to cope calmly and creatively.

handle life as it happens. We focus on healthy, loving relationships; we will always persevere and find our way. This is the time to discuss that spending money isn't what happiness is all about. Help your child to see that a lack of love in life is the greatest struggle.

Listen to their thoughts about money and how they've come to understand it. Don't make it a lecture. Try, if possible, to avoid taking their comments as a judgment about you rather than what it is: a question or a comment on the situation. When times are bad, try not to give in to your bad moods, because that will make your kids avoid the necessary discussions out of a fear that they'll disrupt the emotional stability of the family.

Initiate conversations at leisure times, such as before bed, while cooking, or when going on errands together. Keep in mind that your children are likely to know the level of struggle or change surrounding them, both at home and in their world, even if you don't talk to them about it. They will simply be better equipped to handle it if you *do* talk to them about it.

Yvonne's Story: Camp Miscalculations

I thought that summer camp was the main issue for my children, but I was way off. When my ex-husband told me that he had lost his job, I was mad. Things were complicated enough, and we barely made ends meet as it was. Don't get me wrong—we're not poor. My four kids were in private schools, went to camp regularly, and enjoyed the nice life my ex-husband and I had always wanted for them. I remember that at the time of the divorce, he suddenly wanted the children to go to public school, even though we had paid for private Catholic school every year. It was always a priority for us, and I wasn't going to let my children suffer more changes when I divorced.

I work full-time as an engineer for the city's water department. Even though my ex-husband was supposed to pay half of the school tuition, his job had been cut back, and he was legitimately unable to pay his way for a time. When he was cut back again, however, I asked him to do everything in his power to at least send the kids to the camps they'd been going to for the last few years. Camp was a very important part of my life as a child, and some of my closest friends to this day are friends I made in camp as a child.

Frankly, I also needed a break from the kids in the summer. In order to economize, or so he said, my ex-husband moved in with his mother, to a place that was a two-hour drive away. I didn't care, as long as he paid for camp, but when he lost his job and got a new one in a completely different field that barely paid a living wage, I knew that camp would now be my financial responsibility.

I had to tell the children that everything was going to remain the same in the big things, but that we'd have to live a different daily lifestyle. I thought this was going well, and I was quite proud of myself for managing everything—until my fifteen-year-old asked to talk with me one night after his younger siblings were asleep. He told me that my twelve-year-old, David, didn't want to tell me that he was being teased about his sneakers at school. David was never particularly athletic, like my older son, and he worked very hard to be competitive at sports just so he could fit in. It's odd that sports were so important at a Catholic school, but it was an all-boys' school.

As part of my budget cutting, I had limited certain daily purchases. I had no idea that when David had asked for new sneakers it was that important. In fact, when we had been at the mall earlier that week, David had shown me the sneakers he wanted. They cost $110, and I practically fell over with laughter, thinking he was being ridiculous and spoiled. After all, he knew that his dad had lost his job and everything was falling on me.

Yet David couldn't bring himself to tell me what was happening at school. Apparently he had outgrown his shoes and they hurt, so he wanted the sneakers that everyone was talking about. He kept wearing the expensive sneakers that were too small for him rather than buying new, relatively cheap shoes. Now I had something new to feel completely guilt-ridden about. I couldn't help it. I started to cry right there in front of my fifteen-year-old. I looked off into space and told him how much I wanted things to be the same and how I was trying to save for camp as well, which was quite expensive.

He explained that camp wasn't that important to them; although they loved it, they would much rather have the things in daily life, like new sneakers. My son told me that he'd be just as happy making money as a junior counselor, which he could do because he had attended the camp since he was nine.

Once again, I had a guilty feeling in the pit of my stomach. The thought of him working instead of enjoying his final camp year bothered me more than it bothered him. But he seemed genuinely okay with it and after much explanation I realized that he liked the idea of making his own money to spend the next year as he wished.

My four kids had apparently spoken about it, and they had decided that they'd rather go to a neighborhood day camp or take a little trip with me for a week or so than have the money spent for a whole summer at camp. When I started to consider how much camp cost, I realized how much I could use that money to make their daily lives a little better.

So I ditched the camp idea and got David the sneakers he wanted. He was so relieved. We did take a summer trip, and they spent some time at their grandma's house, so I still got a little break.

Yvonne was dedicated to making her children not feel the sting of recession but wasn't putting her efforts into the right places. Entering your children's world will most likely show you that they have different priorities, some of which you may agree with and some you may not. Until you explore these priorities with them, however, you won't know.

One mother told us that she was going to get her children the next-generation home video game but that the kids preferred to keep the old one and get more games for it. The games for the new one would have been too expensive to buy more than a couple. The kids could get the games for the old one at great discounts online, and they preferred to put the money there. Their parents had felt bad that they couldn't provide the very best. The kids understood and didn't care. Their friends had the new one, so they could play that one when they visited them, but their friends also loved all the old games on the old system, too. Since the friends no longer had the older system, they loved coming over to play it.

Ask Your Children for Their Financial Priorities

When you discuss money with your children, invite them to share what's important to them. Then, as you revise your spending plan, take your kids' priorities into account as well. Like Yvonne, you might be surprised by what is really important to your kids, and their choices may cost you much less than you had planned.

Make Your Children Part of the Family Team

Unfortunately, many of us tell our children to just do well in school—that's their job—and we don't make them feel needed otherwise. We miss the opportunity to make our children feel valued as a result of their contributions to the family. There is nothing wrong and everything right with children being made to feel that their help in the home is crucial to the proper working of the home. Most kids like being made to feel that they are a vital part of the family system. Their opinions about any family matter are important, regardless of the fact that they don't have the final say.

When money was more available, perhaps you didn't need your children to help out as much at home. Maybe you've had to take another job to make ends meet and have less time for meal preparation. Presenting this change to your children does not have to be a mournful moment of looking at good times gone by. You can approach it with the resolution that you're all going to pitch in. There will be changes, but here's what you as a parent are going to be doing. The children can choose the areas they'd most like to help with, or there can be a rotating of chores. If you'll be around less because of more job obligations, the kids may have to hang out with you while you're doing your household chores even though you're used to doing them independently.

One father had his teenagers spend time with him while he balanced the checkbook and did odd jobs around the house. They even accompanied him to work on some days because he had less free time. Before, he had done all of those things by himself, because there was enough time to connect with the kids as a separate activity. However, when his financial life changed and his job demanded more of him for less money, the only time he could grab with the kids was while he was doing other things. So they made it work. He even found it to be an advantage when he realized that he was now teaching them how to manage a checkbook and was talking to them more about himself and his work than ever before. The children liked it, even though at first they had complained.

Don't feel horrible because your children's lives will change. We'd all like to keep life steady, but that is impossible. Teach your children how to deal with life's changes in a healthy, loving way, because they will have to deal with such changes and struggles in life. One of the most important tools to have in life is to be able to stand up to struggle and learn to rise to the occasion.

Accept That Life Has Certain Limitations

When we were kids, we loved superheroes: Superman, Batman— they seemed to have no limits. Yet most kids can tell you each superhero's limit—kryptonite or whatever. (Who knew there was so much kryptonite around?) It seems that we acknowledge the realities of limits even in fantasy scenarios. Children appreciate limits in all things; it makes life predictable. You may feel sad having to impose limits with your children on spending money. We live in a culture that admires celebrities who can spend without limit, but is it good for any child to be raised to think that there are no limits? Doesn't everyone have some limitations?

Gary was explaining this concept recently, and one person replied that there must be *someone* out there who has no limits, someone who can spend any amount that he or she wants. Obviously there are such people: Saudi princes, Microsoft barons, and the like, but even they have limits on how many homes they can enjoy.

We need to become aware of our limitations so that we can make healthy choices. You want to see your bad times as something that causes you to make new choices that perhaps you didn't have to make before, and you should help your child look at it this way, too. Changing your spending habits does not have to be seen as restrictive. It's about choices, no different from the choices that every human being needs to make every day.

We all have to weigh what we spend, whether it's because we have a limited amount of money, because we choose to save more of it, or simply because we want to spend it on something we believe in or enjoy. The idea is to teach your children that financial planning and discussion are about making choices, not about suffering because you can't have everything you wanted or everything you're used to having. Throughout life, we sometimes have more and we sometimes have less.

Don't tell your kids with a sad expression on your face: "We have to tighten our belts." Explain to them the process of life. You choose things based on your present situation. If you have to spend less on certain things now, it's to ensure that the family will have money for vital things. Even if you are not making less money than before, you'd still be wise to choose to spend less, because the world's economy has become so unsure. You shouldn't project gloom and doom to your kids; rather, teach them a sensible life approach about evaluating one's needs versus one's wants.

Have you ever heard your child say, "I need that" when referring to ice cream, a cell phone, a car, a game system, or a laptop? There's no doubt that our indulgence of our children—coming from a good place, of course—has blurred the line between needs and wants for them. So many of us have allowed our kids to believe that it really is a lot of stuff that makes one happy. The current weak economy is our chance to redeem ourselves and become better parents who teach our kids to invest in relationships, to value love, to develop their talents, and to find ways of using those talents to improve the world. It's love and a sense of purpose in life that make us happy, and our kids can learn that in the most sincere way.

Sally's Story: Family Hurricane Nights

Living in South Florida, we've been through our share of hurricanes. Within an hour of even the mildest of hurricanes hitting, the electricity goes out. I'm sure most people have experienced that for an evening or so. In my apartment complex, it happens quickly, and we are always ready with our candles and games. We get ready with board games, cards, and books.

Every time, we have a blast. The children and my husband and I talk and laugh. We tell stories about our parents. It's the only time that everyone's cell phone isn't ringing and that the computer is off, the video games are off, and the television is silent. After the lights come back on, even my kids always say the same thing: Why don't we do that more often?

After the money problems we've been having, I really thought we were falling into some kind of [emotional] depression. I decided one Friday night that we'd make a "hurricane night." At first everyone, even my husband, complained, but I persevered, and we did it for just one hour. It was great. We have now done it for two hours, one night a week, for six weeks in a row. It was like pulling teeth the first few times, but now my kids remind me in the morning that tonight is "hurricane night." One of my kids loves to cook, so he prepares dinner that night; another is always finding a new card game to play. It has really become our time to reconnect, and I suggest it for everyone. Turn the lights off, turn everything off, and just be with your family.

The Financial Conversation with Your Kids

Discussing financial shifts and changes involves thinking aloud as a family unit, making your children aware of the changes in your lives, and opening the topic for discussion. It's your chance as a parent to put your children's minds at ease, to let them know the specific things that are going on, and to reassure them lovingly.

You might frame your conversation as follows:

1. Explain reality and the changes that have occurred

> We want to talk to you about some things that are happening in the financial world. As you know, the world has changed and companies are closing. This situation affects everyone, because when people stop having money, there's less to spend, and others have less business. Just about everyone is making some changes in how they spend their money. In our case, we [choose all relevant statements]: have seen our home values go down; have seen our stock portfolio go down; have lost our jobs; have had a reduction in pay; have to work much harder to make the same or less money; are about the same moneywise but are concerned about the future; have a great deal and want to find ways as a family to give to others.

2. Reassure them

> We want you to know that we're on top of this, and although we can't promise what will happen moneywise,

we are still going to be okay. We're a family, and stuff happens, but we will deal with it. There are things to be grateful for: we have our health [if this is true in your case], and most important, we really do love one another. Having that to depend on is everything. More or less money won't change how we feel about one another.

3. Suggest changes in money-spending choices (these will obviously change depending on your situation).

> We will need to make some new choices. A lot of times in life, you have to make new decisions based on what happens in your life and the world. Just as you may want to take dance and karate lessons, but they're happening at the same time, so you have to make a choice, we have to make choices as a family. For example, as your parents, we have to make sure that we have enough money to pay for our home, our food, our clothes, and our visits to the doctor. That's our responsibility, and we don't want you to ever have to worry about that. In order for us to be able to take care of this, we have to choose to keep our money for the most important things.

> We are considering making some changes, including [This is a nicer phrase than just bluntly saying that you are making changes. Ease your children into it, and after you hear from them, you may reconsider some things.] spending less by [state two or three items and no more the first time so you don't overwhelm them]: not taking that vacation we were planning; spending

less on clothing; cutting out our household services; finding a job; working more hours, which will mean we'll be around a bit less for the time being. Let's talk about how we can make these changes as comfortable as possible for all of us.

[If you might have to move, add the following.] We might choose to move to a more affordable situation, and although we know this is a big change that we weren't planning on and would prefer not to make, we'll work together to make it as pleasant as possible. Let's talk about how we can make it work for us.

4. Open the conversation for them so they can tell you what's important to them

   We wanted to ask you what your thoughts are. What things would you most like to stay the same? Let's see what we can do to try to work together to make things best for all of us under these circumstances.

5. Ask them for their suggestions

   Do you guys have any suggestions about the choices we make? [Stay away from saying what they could do to help, because that can put too much pressure on them. You already made some suggestions about changes and about ways they might have to help, so there is no need to do that now.]

6. Reassure them again and commit yourselves to continuing the conversation in the future

   We're having this conversation because we're working together as a family to grow through this situation and to make sure that the important things are with us and that we'll be okay. We need to focus on what we have and think about the people who have it so much worse than we do. We can still be happy that we have one another and be grateful for the love in our family. You kids are great, and of course we'd prefer that everything always stay perfect, but life isn't like that. The important thing is for us to keep talking about things and try to be kind to one another.

7. End with the following:

There are some things we don't know for sure and some things we do know for sure. We don't know for sure what will happen in the future with regard to our money. We do know for sure that we'll always love you, and we'll have lots of good times as long as we keep focusing on the love we have in this family. We under-stand that this could be kind of scary, confusing, and sad for you, but that's why we're discussing it.

The Most Important Listening Technique to Help Children

As we have already mentioned, you don't have to be the parent with all the answers. As a matter of fact, it's often a bad idea to act as if you have all the answers even if you do. When a child asks a question or makes a statement, it's often not a good idea to give a quick answer without taking the time to understand what is behind the question or the statement. Much more important than the script in the previous section is the response you'll have to your children's comments.

Because we are loving parents, we tend to answer our children too quickly in order to protect them. We don't want to see them sad or confused, so we work hard to immediately alleviate any negative feelings.

What if during your financial discussion, your ten-year-old son says, "Why do we have to stay in this house? Can't we move and save money?" The common parental answer would be to swoop in and make the child feel better. It's awful that this child is trying to convince his parents to move out of a house to save money, isn't it? So you might say, "No, don't worry. We're fine. We have the money for the house." This reply ends the conversation before you've had the chance to explore your child's thoughts. Your desire to rescue him from sadness triggered an answer to his question instead of a further understanding of what he was feeling.

One mother tried to imagine how her child was feeling and said, "You're kind of worried that if we stay in the house, we'll lose all our money, aren't you?"

Her son responded, "Yeah, because Tommy said his parents are getting a divorce because they stayed in the house too long, and they have to sell it now and live in two different places."

The mother wasn't quite sure what Tommy was thinking or what her son had heard, but by using a simple listening technique she discovered a whole world of anxiety behind her son's seemingly innocent suggestion.

Perhaps your daughter will hear the two of you fighting and ask her father, "Are you and Mommy fighting about money?"

You may want to say, "No, we're fine," but if you've been fighting, lying doesn't help your cause. Imagine saying instead, "It sounds as if you're concerned about us getting along." This sends a warm, understanding message to her that you really do understand what's going on inside her. You can then use another important parental technique: stop talking and give your child a chance to respond.

"I heard you call Dad a bad name," your daughter says to her mother.

Now you've gotten much deeper into what is concerning her. She'll need to act out less and will be less upset in general because she is finding a proper form of expression for her complicated feelings.

You could help her express herself even further with a response such as, "It must be somewhat upsetting to hear me talk like that to Dad." Here again, you've helped her to "get out" some feelings that are very hard to deal with. You've understood her, and she can learn to explore these emotions and bring them to you.

What if she then responds with "I was upset because I know Daddy screamed at you, and I don't want the two of you fighting all the time."

Imagine the greater communication you've fostered because your daughter was able to explore and express her feelings as a result of your ability to listen and understand instead of simply jumping in to make her feel better.

There is always time to reassure and give a detailed answer, and you should do both—at the end of the conversation, when neither of you has anything else to say and you're sure that your daughter has exhausted her need to express herself. You say, "Look, I'm sorry that you have had this experience. Even adults make mistakes and say things they shouldn't, but Dad and I are doing okay, and we'll work harder to speak nicely to each other."

The mother in the earlier example could say to her son, "We can afford this house, and we are not getting divorced."

At this point, agree to revisit the conversation, give your child permission to bring up any upsetting feelings in the future, and do your best to make the healthy changes your child has suggested.

The point of your conversation with your children is not to deny their feelings of sadness. We certainly don't mean to imply that you should be dancing around with some false happiness about the changes you'll have to make. But don't give your children a sense of doom and gloom, either. They will follow your lead, so as long as they sense that you're in control and are making sure that the basic needs are cared for, their anxiety level will be greatly diminished.

Let's just recognize their concern and bring it up to them. If they are unresponsive, you can say, "I know this is kind of difficult for you, and we understand that you're upset about it." Again, stop yourself from immediately reassuring your children, and give them the opportunity to get in touch with their feelings and share their thoughts with you.

Put Yourself in Their Shoes

The best communication stems from your ability as a parent to put yourself into the perspective of a child. Imagine how your children of various ages may be feeling, and feel it to the best of your ability. Once you do that, your response will be a comment of true understanding.

Always take a moment at first to respond to anything serious your children say by feeling what they might be feeling and letting them know that this is what you think they are feeling. However, use gentle feelings, because it's often hard for any of us to admit that we're feeling intense emotions. If your spouse said to you, "You must be really mad at your boss," you might reduce it a notch, saying, "I'm not sure I'm really mad, just annoyed." You might appreciate hearing something like "I can understand your being somewhat upset at your boss." That's a much more palatable message for most people. Use words like *sort of, kind of, maybe, rather, a little,* or *a bit* before stating the feeling you believe a child is feeling. Doing so will allow your children to continue describing their feelings with another comment rather than getting into subtle disagreements over how they really feel.

Imagine the following conversation with your son:

He: "I can't believe we're not going to the same school next year."

You: "I can understand that might be somewhat upsetting."

He: "Well, yeah, I was set to be a starter for the basketball team."

You: "And you've worked hard for two years to get to this point."

He: "I put in my time and sat on the bench year after year just to get to this point, and now you're ripping it away from me!"

You: "I'm sorry about all of this. It really is a shame, but it's nothing anyone could foresee. It sounds as if you think we could do this differently."

At this point, the anger of most children (even teenagers) will have subsided, because they see and can feel that you get them. When we hear that someone is sorry about a situation, it helps us to get past our anger. Truly understanding your child reduces the intensity of a feeling and dissipates anger. In the case just mentioned, an ensuing conversation could be an explanation of why private school is no longer affordable or why moving is a necessity.

A child's feelings may cause you to reconsider your decision. If you learn that basketball was a serious pursuit or a possible vehicle by which your son could attend college, you might find another way to accomplish your financial cuts. It may cause you to help your son get in touch with the next coach at the new school and arrange a special tryout if tryouts have passed. Perhaps his present coach could become involved. The conversation continues from above:

He: "I dunno. I'd sure love to start next year, that's all."

You: "Let's not lose that thought. Let's think about getting you into that position, whether here or in your new school. Does the new school have a competitive team?"

He: "I think so. But I'd have to find out if college scouts come to see it. I was wondering if I was good enough to get into college on a scholarship."

The conversation thus proceeds in a productive manner.

You can help your child to create a possible resolution to a problem instead of worrying about how the conversation would have gone had you not worked to understand the child's feelings.

Here's a negative take on the same conversation:

He: "I can't believe I'm not going to the same school next year."

You: "Well, we all have to make sacrifices."

He: "Why don't you make some sacrifices? You could buy a cheaper car and stop getting expensive clothing. I bet that would help."

You: "How dare you tell me how to live my life! I'm the parent here! How much of a spoiled brat can you be?"

He: "Takes one to know one!"

Ah, the adolescent. This conversation was doomed because the parent became defensive, taking an "I'm the parent and that's all that matters" attitude. Feeling bad about the son's anger, the parent simply stated that everyone has to make sacrifices. The parent is correct, but there is a more constructive way to respond to the adolescent's sense of disappointment. When the teenager lashed out and asked why the parent wasn't making more sacrifices, the parent should have tried to be the "adult" in the situation and respond calmly (perhaps with an example of a sacrifice that he or she was indeed making) rather than exploding into "I'm the parent and don't you dare talk to me that way!" Understanding a teenager's feelings and setting limits that demand respectful exchanges are not mutually exclusive. "I understand your disappointment," the parent could say, "and I'm willing to discuss it, but you need to have a better tone for us to have an honest conversation about it."

Imagine now this gentler approach:

He: "I can't believe I'm not going to the same school next year."

You: "I'm so sorry about this. I feel horrible. Please try to understand; it'll be okay. We'll get through this as a family, and these changes will help us to have a better financial future."

This rescuing, reassuring comment is also defensive, however. Filled with guilt, it destroys the conversation and leaves no room for any productive resolution. The parent is basically saying, I'm so guilty about this, I can't even touch it, so let's please stop talking about it, and it'll be okay. Don't feel the way you're feeling, and let's just say it'll all be okay, okay? The teen will still act out and be angry.

Don't worry about your feelings so much when your children talk to you. Don't immediately personalize it and feel so awful about the fact that your children are experiencing sad or perceived negative feelings. Just put yourself in their shoes and let yourself feel their feelings, even if you are the one who might be the cause of those feelings. "It's understandable that this would be disappointing for you," gives children the sense that they're understood, offering them the opportunity to communicate their feelings.

Here is a final example:

A nine-year-old boy and his fourteen-year-old sister had heard about the financial issues their single mother was having. As part of her explanation about her stocks falling, she said, "I wish I had just put it all in the bank, although who knows if the banks will even be safe? Maybe we should put all our money in the mattress," she continued in a quasi-joking manner.

Her son became visibly distraught.

"What's the matter, honey?" Mom asked.

The boy thought intensely. "Don't I have money in the bank?" he asked, referring to the $220 he had put in the bank on his last birthday. He had even continued to add to it a little here and there.

She set him straight by replying, "Oh, don't be ridiculous. That money is safe, and even if there's a problem, I'd always be able to give you that amount of money. Don't worry."

The nine-year-old burst into tears and ran off to his room. His mother followed him, held him and made more reassuring comments.

Let's back up and listen better.

"What's the matter, honey?" Mom asked.

The boy thought intensely. "Don't I have money in the bank?"

"You're worried about your money?"

"What if you run out and we need it?"

Now her son was offering a much deeper problem that had not been answered before, when Mom explained that she would reimburse him if he lost his money. He wasn't worried about losing his money but rather hers. Now Mom can reassure him about the issue that is really pressing for him.

> "Oh, I think I understand now. You're worried we'll run out of everything. That's why we're talking about it. I'm making sure we won't run out of it. And that comment I made about the banks was really more of a joke. So far, the banks have been fine, and the government secures the amount of money we have in our bank accounts so that people can get their money out even if there is a more serious problem."

Here's another possibility:

> "What's the matter, honey?" Mom asked.
> The boy thought intensely. "Don't I have money in the bank?"
> "So you're kind of scared about losing the money you've saved?"
> "No, not really. But Grandma once told me she puts all of her money in the bank and keeps it safe there. Maybe we should tell her to take it all out. What if Grandma doesn't have enough money?"

Again, Mom discovered a deeper, more important message from her son that she could not have found if she had simply jumped in to reassure him, as she first did. It was her guilt and her understandable discomfort with her son being in any kind of distress—especially because of something she had said or because of her perceived failure of not having enough money—that motivated her to solve the problem for him. In doing so, however, she cut him off and didn't give him an opportunity to express himself or even discover what was bothering him.

Listening to Your Child

1. Put yourself in your child's shoes.
2. First respond with the feeling that you think your child is experiencing.
3. Put *kind of, sort of,* or *a bit* before the feeling: "It sounds as though you feel a bit scared."
4. Hold back from saying anything more and give your child a chance to continue the thought.
5. Help your child to consider how to resolve the feeling.
6. Don't rescue, feel guilty, apologize, or make the conversation about your feelings, because then you'll be ending the conversation. You can always do this at a later point, even if it's one or two minutes later.
7. Reassure your child, knowing that the conversation is coming to an end.

Sometimes the children themselves don't yet know what's bothering them, and they need to have an open conversation with their parents as a sounding board to help them get in touch with it. These needs are no different from what adults often need from family, friends, and therapists. Remember that you can always rescue your child with a reassuring comment or a loving gesture—and you should do that. Kids thrive on it. Do it, however, when there's nothing else to say, because once you've done it, you've effectively closed the conversation.

Children Talk the Most When You Least Expect It

The best way to shut down any communication with your children is to look them straight in the eyes and bring up a difficult question like "How are you feeling about the money talk we had?" Communication is always most comfortable in a relaxed, no-pressure setting. Kids tend to broach complicated and uncomfortable feelings and questions when there is a relaxed atmosphere, such as riding in the car, tossing a baseball, or getting ready to go to asleep. These are moments when they also sense that you are relaxed and have a calm moment to be there for them. Create little quiet moments with your children in this way as often as possible. What's important is not the big expensive times but rather all the small, loving moments, when your children have your full attention and thus feel able to really open up.

Safety in Numbers

Help your child realize that others are experiencing similar situations. Children rarely like to be different from others. Even though the media pound away on the topic of money during a recession, it doesn't mean that your child recognizes that most families are cutting spending or having these kinds of conversations. There is tremendous safety for your children in knowing that they are not alone and that your family is similar to everyone else's family, who in tough economic times chooses to make spending changes. Explain to your child that many people keep their financial affairs private, so other children may not be comfortable discussing the issue of money or sharing what's going on in their families. Your children might not even be aware of other kids' needs to deal with similar changes.

Initiate the Conversation Rather Than Waiting for Them to Come to You

Too many parents say, "If you have any feelings about it, you can always come to me and talk about it." It's a really nice thought, but rarely in history has that statement led a child to approach a parent to discuss complicated feelings.

Connecting is the key to love and something that you can't wait for a child to initiate. We heal through loving connections. Even as adults, the experience of merely connecting with another is magical. Someone could be dying of a life-threatening disease, and talking to a friend about it for half an hour can make her feel better. Her disease is no less deadly, but she still feels better because the experience of connecting with another human being and feeling as if someone understands her is healing.

Invite your child to express his or her emotions—expressing them is the healthiest way to begin working them out. Don't try to hide from your children's hurt by avoiding the conversation or rescuing them from their feelings. As humans, we need touch, hugs, loving words, and affectionate gestures to survive.

Financial issues can benefit you and your family. If you come out of them with children who have become skilled at understanding the deeper meaning of love and family, you'll look back one day and say, "My kids have real coping skills; good came out of this." Your children could never have understood these lessons without this experience. Being open and not making the situation a frightening one will allow your children to grow up not fearing money but seeing it as the reality it is—a necessary item to get certain things—and not confusing it with love.

When your children experience your family living life and having fun, learning and growing together, spending meaningful time together, hanging out and being one another's support, they will learn that the most important things in life don't require money. Nor do they wait for anything. Your children are young and this impressionable only once. You can make it count by showing them how true family love works. It'll be a positive lesson that they will draw on for the rest of their lives.

Can You Spare a Down Payment?
When Adult Children or
Parents Need Help

Parents today continue to be involved in their children's lives way beyond the age of eighteen or twenty-one. Many parents are called upon or just feel a desire to be of help financially. Others, like Amy and Timothy from the *Oprah* show, relied on her parents when the marriage was breaking up and they lost their house. Amy's mother provided a home and child care for her daughter, thus allowing Amy to work.

Some adult children find that their parents need help, perhaps for the first time in their parents' lives.

Evaluating the situation and being clear and loving in your communication helps to establish what you can do for one another. The stress can be difficult no matter who is making the changes. Here are some guidelines:

- Let go of guilt. You are not defined by what you give.

- Clearly communicate what you think you can provide: "We can continue to help with your rent. We can't continue to pay for your cell phone, car insurance, and the extras."

- Set boundaries: "We love you and love babysitting for the grandchildren. We'll need a day's notice, though, so we can see if we're available—unless it's an emergency."

- When sharing living quarters, set up expectations ahead of time: cooking, grocery shopping, who pays which bills, and who watches the children when. These should all be agreed upon to avoid any hurt feelings later.

- Seek outside support if you're getting stressed out. Life changes within the family can trigger feelings from other times. If you find yourself becoming tense, or you just need to alleviate stress, discuss the issues with a friend you trust or with a professional.

- Give notice when possible. Say something like "We've been going over our accounts, and we need to let you know that we can continue giving you only [fill in amount] for another two months. You need to look into other options. Let us know if you need our help in looking into these options."

Our messages to children of all ages need to be straightforward and loving. Children need to feel that they are part of the family team at any stage. It's always better to be up front and not send mixed messages. Being direct will set up the relationship for successful communication about any struggle.

10

Family Fun That Won't Bust the Bank

South Beach, Florida, in the early 1980s was not a place in which you'd find Madonna or Diddy. The neighborhood was a hub for the narcotics industry. Many of the buildings were run-down, with broken windows and boarded-up doorways. In the few years we lived there, the neighborhood went through so much change it was staggering. An Armani Exchange replaced a Laundromat overnight.

Because Gary's grandparents' vacant condo was in South Beach, we inserted ourselves in this upheaval and acclimated ourselves and our two babies to it. We found some rather colorful characters at the time, because the neighborhood had not yet become gentrified.

Jo Anne and Craig were our age. They lived in an understated but decent apartment near Lincoln Road. It was a simple place, and we figured that they had income but no extra money. In fact, they were just people who were spending only on what was part of their personal value system. They had money to waste but chose not to do so. This drove home to us the message that a lot of what is seen as deprivation might in fact be an opportunity to live more consciously. You could waste money or go into debt to acquire things and have fun, or you could enjoy yourself for less without feeling deprived.

Jo Anne and Craig, and people like them, are the key to a different perspective. Whether or not you have money, there's a place in your life for fun, and it can be redefined. Fun doesn't have to involve spending; it can be about finding ways of enjoying ourselves and others without spending much or wasting money.

Some of the following advice applies only to those who live in cities, and some applies to those who live in the country; some applies to couples, and some to families. The point of all of it is to network and be creative in what you are willing to consider. *Change the mind-set from deprivation to one of choice.* Having fun is largely a mind-set and varies according to the individual. It is important to have nice times.

In the next several pages, we list some good starting points, but fun and entertainment are so based on personal taste that there can't really be any universally applicable list. Visiting museums and sitting quietly at free concerts won't do it for the hyperactive of any generation. The key is creativity and awareness. Planning a garage sale, canning produce, and singing are all activities that will be hailed as great fun by some people and will produce elitist snickers in others. (You know who you are.)

Find what works for you and be open to new experiences together. Make the time to do something that makes life good for you and for others.

Here are some fun family activities (many are even free):

- Visiting museums and art galleries

- Attending lectures or adult education classes at universities, colleges, or public schools

- Attending religious gatherings or adult education classes at your local church or temple

- Going to book talks at a local bookstore. You don't have to buy the book.

- Swimming

- Hiking together as a family

- Talking to one another. Make a date to talk about a specific topic or event.

- Entertaining your friends at home. Have a get-together for a cause or just a casual party. Gatherings are healthy and fun. People can bring food or take turns hosting.

- Starting a film club for couples. Show movies that both men and women will like.

- Volunteering to make a difference. This is the single most life-changing thing you can do for yourselves as a couple and for your children. We have visited the same nursing home for thirteen years, and we sometimes go to other cities and visit the nursing homes there. Sometimes we bring doughnuts, homemade cookies, or flowers. My teenagers play cards with some men who have a lot of stories to tell. It is a truly amazing experience, and there is no better lesson for your kids in practicing kindness. Visiting a hospital and talking to patients who would like visitors can be equally meaningful. Feeding and helping the homeless is so important and gives everyone involved a feeling of great purpose. There are usually local organizations that help the homeless that are thrilled to have others involved. Become part of a charitable organization and give as much time as you, your partner, and your kids want to give.

- Going on a date in a fancy hotel lobby

- Having a drink in a club with live music.

- Going to auctions. The auction house we visited in the woods of upstate New York was incredibly fun. Check out http://www.auctionzip.com to find out about auctions in your area. You can see rare things that are sold for thousands, yet you can also buy something for a dollar. We really enjoyed it. There are usually items for sale for every age range. Some auctions serve homemade food.

- Going to sample sales and trunk shows. These are city events at which designer clothes are sold.

- Going to auto shows, boat shows, and orchid shows. Admission is often nominal and the different people, settings, and items can spark discussions and take you out of your comfort zone.

- Debating with others. Nicholas Kristof wrote a great piece in the *New York Times* in which he lamented the loss of the genuine exchange of different points of view in discourse.

Speaking to and listening to opinions and worldviews that differ from your own can add to your storehouse of knowledge and serve as a springboard for interesting and entertaining conversation. If you're an intellectual from the East Coast, getting out of your comfort zone and attending a country music festival or a rodeo can be a lot of fun. If you're from a small town in Missouri or a cattle ranch in Texas, attend a lecture on a topic with which you disagree. Obviously, we aren't talking about doing something that you find truly threatening or with which you have a deep philosophical problem. Seeking out other experiences and conversation, however, is good mental exercise.

- Taking a trip to the Apple Store. For an annual fee of ninety nine dollars, you can receive one-to-one computer tutoring. You don't have to own a Macintosh computer; you just schedule the sessions and learn new computer things. It's a great weekly date night or family event.

- Attending indoor and outdoor concerts

- Creating classes with other couples or families. One group of women arranged to have a weekly yoga instructor. She charged her hourly rate, and the women split the cost.

- Going antiques shopping. Even people who dislike shopping often find it fun to look through things from long ago. Sometimes the dealers will tell you the history of the piece or some obscure bit of information; sometimes it's just interesting to see the stuff you played with as a kid being sold as a rare collectible. Everyone seems happy at antiques shows, and towns lined with antiques shops are a lot of fun. Gary looks for names on paintings and searches the Internet for them with his BlackBerry, waiting and hoping for that proud moment he can be on PBS's *Antiques Roadshow*, saying, "What? I can't believe it's worth that! I found it at an antiques shop for fifty cents!" He has not yet found the perfect item, but he has learned about many artists and has shared the information about their fascinating lives with the kids.

- Motorboating, sailing, riding all-terrain vehicles, and parasailing. These are all exciting activities to share with other people and divide the cost. We know one man who shares an all-terrain vehicle with his friend. You can rent unusual equipment or enjoy these activities especially during off-peak hours.

- Joining a chess club. You can often join one at a library, or you can start your own.

- Taking your kid to other people's workplaces. It's surprising how welcoming workplaces can be to other people's children. Many places—for example, the fire station (ask for a plastic red fire hat), the bank, the bakery—will give you a tour and explain how things work there if they aren't busy.

- Going to art festivals

- Going to cultural festivals. Search your local newspaper for events.

- Playing sports. Consider the sports or activities that gave you pleasure at other stages of your life, and see if they still appeal to you now. Tennis, walking, or softball, anyone? Getting together with people outside your generation is a good way to enjoy new experiences. Be open to the kid who wants to take you sailing or the teenager who wants to show you a dance-dance revolution game. Perhaps an older couple will take you dancing.

- Asking "connectors" about fun events. Malcolm Gladwell wrote about connectors in his best-selling book *The Tipping Point: How Little Things Can Make a Big Difference.* These are the people who know everyone. They aren't gossips; they just seem to inspire trust and know a large number of people. They're great to consult with for all kinds of information, but especially for interesting and fun events. They also seem to know value and how to qualify for better seats at the special introductory rate. Think of anyone you know who fits this description and have a talk with him or her about the activities in your area.

- Cooking and making crafts. Use these activities as a springboard for sharing and communication with your kids. Remember that kids always share best in an informal, unpressured setting. Have fun with homemade play dough, tea party scones, bread in the shape of a bear, gingerbread houses, and oil-burning menorahs. If only we had known before we spent ten million dollars on preschool that all you really need are googly eyes from the craft store and a bottle of glue! Weekends are long, and these classic activities are universally appealing. Little boys whom you are actively watching for the warning signs of a personality problem will smile and look joyful making bread bears. Little girls will stop talking on their tiny pink cell phones to join in. I know teenagers who were delighted to be invited to their church's knitting group; they found a new hobby. Knitting is now in with many teens.

Fun and Easy Recipes

Here are some of our favorite recipes to make as a family.

Homemade Play Dough

3 cups flour

1½ cups salt

6 teaspoons cream of tartar

3 cups cool water

3 tablespoons oil

Food coloring

Mix the dry ingredients in a big pot. Blend the liquids in a bowl. Combine the wet and the dry ingredients and cook over medium heat, stirring constantly. Remove from heat when the dough pulls away from the sides of the pot and can be pinched without sticking (about 5 minutes). Turn onto a board or the counter and knead until the consistency is smooth. Store in an airtight container.

Bread Bears

This recipe is reprinted with permission from The Complete Tightwad Gazette: Promoting Thrift as a Viable Alternative Lifestyle *by Amy Dacyczyn.*

One package dry yeast

¼ cup warm water

½ cup softened butter

$1/4$ to $1/2$ cup honey
3 teaspoons grated lemon peel
1 teaspoon pure almond extract
3 teaspoons lemon juice
$1/2$ teaspoon salt
3 eggs, plus 3 eggs separated
$1/2$ cup warm milk
5 to 6 cups unbleached flour
Cinnamon sugar

Combine the yeast with the water. Stir with a fork until dissolved and set aside.

In a large bowl using an electric mixer, cream the next five ingredients. Mix until fluffy. Beat in the eggs and the egg yolks one at a time (reserve the three egg whites for the glaze). With a spatula blend in the milk and the yeast mixture.

Beat in two cups of flour to make a smooth batter. Add enough flour to make a stiff dough.

Turn the dough onto a lightly floured surface. Knead it until the texture is smooth, about ten minutes. Place the dough in a buttered bowl, cover lightly with a cloth, and allow it to rise in a warm place for an hour or until doubled in bulk.

Turn the dough onto a lightly floured surface, punch it down, and let it rest for ten minutes.

To assemble the bears:

Each recipe makes two twelve-inch bears or four eight-inch bears or you can make a number of small ones. Divide your dough into disks, one for each bear.

Bread Bears (continued)

Divide each disk in half. One half makes the body. Divide the second half into sections. One section becomes the head. The remaining section is used for bear body parts. Pull off a quarter of it to make a bear nose. The remainder of the dough is divided in half. The first half into thirds—one for the two ears and two for the arms. The last section is divided in half to make two legs. Roll the body section into a smooth ball and place in the center of a greased cookie sheet and flatten slightly. Roll the head section smooth and attach it to the body. (Use a small amount of water to stick together bear parts.) Roll the nose and ear sections and attach them. The arm and leg sections are rolled into cylinders and attached.

To finish the bear, press indentations with your index finger to make eyes and a belly button. Put a blanched nut in each eye socket so it will hold its shape while baking.

Cover the bear with a clean cloth in a draft-free space. Preheat the oven to 375 degrees F. Beat one egg white with one teaspoon of water. Using a pastry brush, paint the entire top surface of the bear with the egg glaze. Sprinkle with cinnamon sugar (to make cinnamon sugar mix one half cup granulated sugar with one teaspoon cinnamon). Bake the bears, 30 to 45 minutes or until golden brown (smaller bears take less time). After baking remove the nuts from the eyes. Let cool for one hour. Place raisins or candies in the eyes.

Tie brightly colored ribbon around the bear's neck. Place a large bear on a piece of foil-covered cardboard and cover with plastic wrap. Or put several small bears in a basket.

Tea Party Scones

This recipe appeals to adults and children alike.

1½ cups flour
1 tablespoon baking powder
6 teaspoons sugar
½ teaspoon salt
¾ cup butter (plus some extra to grease the pan)
½ cup milk
1 egg yolk
Jam or clotted cream (optional)

Preheat the oven to 375 degrees F.

Combine the dry ingredients. Then, using a knife or your hands, crumble the butter into the flour mixture until the flour resembles coarse meal. Add the milk and mix. Knead the dough for just a minute. Take a palm-sized piece of dough and roll it into a ball. Push the center in to create an indentation. Repeat with the rest of the dough.

Place the scones on a buttered cookie sheet 3 to 5 inches apart. Brush with the egg yolk. Bake for about 25 minutes. Serve with jam (strawberry is good). These scones are also often served with clotted cream, a rich topping that can be found in some specialty stores.

Gingerbread House

This can be a wonderful family project, done over several days. It can serve as a holiday centerpiece, a special gift, or an addition to a class party. Kids of every age, even toddlers, can participate. It's truly a fun and lighthearted activity. Virtually any type of candy can be added, and the royal icing can be used as edible glue.

You can make gingerbread ski lodges, cottages, toy factories, or whatever you like. Fancy molds can be purchased through the Internet, or walls can be rolled out by hand.

GINGERBREAD

1 cup butter or margarine, softened

4 large eggs

1 cup brown sugar

1 cup white sugar

1 cup dark molasses

5 cups flour (plus extra for rolling)

1 teaspoon ginger

1½ teaspoons cinnamon

1 teaspoon ginger

½ teaspoon nutmeg

1 teaspoon cloves

2 teaspoons baking soda

½ teaspoon salt

½ to ¾ cup water

ROYAL ICING

Yield: 6 cups

1 pound powdered sugar
5 tablespoons meringue powder or ¼ cup pasteurized egg whites
2 tablespoons water
Food coloring (optional)

Preheat the oven to 375 degrees F. In a large mixing bowl beat the butter or margarine. Add the eggs one at a time and beat well. Add the sugars and beat until fluffy, at least 2 minutes. Add the molasses and beat on medium for another two to four minutes.

Combine the flour, spices, baking soda, and salt, then add them to the wet ingredients a little at a time, mixing as you add. At the same time also add the water to make the mixing easier. You will have to use your hands to work the dough toward the end.

Divide the dough into thirds and shape into balls. Cover with plastic wrap and chill for several hours, preferably overnight.

Roll out one ball into a sheet about ½-inch thick. Chill on a baking pan or foil. You can also dust your hands with flour and press the dough into a rectangular shape. (This method will result in less professional-looking walls but life is too short to worry about it.) Repeat three times until you have four walls. Then make one more sheet and cut in half. This will be the roof. Carve any designs you like into the dough at this point. Then slide the walls onto cookie sheets and bake them for about fifteen minutes. Check on them after ten minutes.

Gingerbread House (continued)

When all the pieces have finished baking, remove them from the oven. As soon as the pieces come out of the oven, check the edges and, if necessary, trim with a sharp knife so that the pieces will fit together. Allow them to cool on the cookie sheets.

Allow the gingerbread plenty of time to cool on the cookie sheets before you begin construction. If you can't start building right away, slide the fully cooled pieces back onto the cookie sheets, wrap with foil or plastic wrap, and store flat. Gingerbread will stay reasonably fresh for several days.

For the icing, combine the powdered sugar and the meringue powder or egg whites in a mixing bowl and beat with an electric mixer on low speed. Add the water one drop at a time. The amount you will need to use depends on whether you used meringue powder or egg whites and on the temperature and humidity in your kitchen. Add the water slowly and do not let the mixture become runny; you will probably not use all of the water. Beat until the mixture holds a trail on the surface of the icing for five seconds when you raise the mixer from the bowl. If you like, you can tint the icing with a few drops of food coloring.

When it's time to assemble the house, choose a surface that will hold the construction and any additional decorations. Use the royal icing liberally to glue the walls together. There are many building tips and templates available on the Internet, as well as many gingerbread enthusiasts who offer their tips to make your experience a special one. (Type A personalities be warned.) Don't get frustrated if your walls fall down; use cans or other objects to prop them up until the icing has set. Using marzipan, vegetable shortening, and candy, you can create a lot of different themes and characters to sit outside the house. Glue candy to the house or sprinkle with confectioner's sugar.

Menorah Oil Lights

This Hanukkah menorah is unusual for kids. Instead of using candles, it uses oil to burn, which duplicates the original holiday theme (when a cruse of oil burned in the Temple for eight days).

In a row, line up eight small juice glasses, shot glasses, or other small glasses. Fill each glass three-fourths full with water and add food coloring for decoration. Add two or three tablespoons of olive oil or vegetable oil per glass. For wicks, you have two options. You can twist cotton threads into a thin wick, place one end in the glass, and light the other. You could also just use "floating wicks," which are very cool and extremely inexpensive. These can be ordered through www.eichlers.com or www.judaism.com. Line up the glasses on a table or attach them, using Krazy Glue, to a clay or ceramic candleholder.

11

Making Holidays Better in Good Times and Bad

Holidays are special times when you gather with your family or friends; ideally, at the end of your time together, you are left with valuable memories. For some people it's the thoughtful gift brought by a relative; for others it's the spiritual inspiration of reconnecting with friends.

Holidays are tricky because they involve long-standing traditions, people's feelings, childhood issues, unrequited love, and/or lost chances. A whole airport conveyor belt of emotional baggage can come sliding out around a holiday, and change, with all its attendant fears and anxieties, can be hard to implement.

For some people, holidays are no big deal. Others find them a bit much because of all there is to do: the exhaustion involved in the preparations, the endless search for gifts, and the cooking and serving of a large meal (which may be underappreciated). Then there are the family dynamics: the nephew who wants to see what will happen if he "frees" your tropical fish from their tank ("He loves to experiment," his mother beams at you as you scramble to retrieve the gasping fish); the well-meaning relative ("I got you the extra large sweater, dear. I surely hope it's big enough"); and your Aunt Ida who—no, did she just put your

Making Holidays Work

Reexamine how you spend your holidays and see what works and what doesn't.

1. Take the time to prepare. Review your plans with someone else so you can hear yourself discussing them aloud and hear how they sound—it's worth it. Last-minute tasks always translate to stress that can set the stage for disaster.
2. Make a list of things you personally like about the holiday.
3. Make a list of things that bother you about the holiday and creatively find ways to change these. Give yourself permission to enjoy the holiday.
4. Do the math in advance. How much is this going to cost you? Are you sure you're okay with it? Otherwise, find ways to cut your expenses.

china candy dish in her purse? Well yes, she does that sort of thing, and everybody just pretends not to notice. Add any sort of stress, like a financial upheaval or a lost job, and the whole celebration goes from good time to bad faster than you can say, "Charge it." What can you do?

There really isn't much you can control about holidays except for yourself. Taking good care of yourself by getting enough sleep, breathing deeply, and not falling into the little traps of family dynamics can all help. Examining—with your partner, a friend, a clergyperson, or a therapist—the stressful feelings that can come up at holiday times goes a long way toward helping you to have a good time.

Reexamine How You Spend Your Holidays

Sometimes, going through a bad time gives you the permission you need to radically alter your way of celebrating. One family we know, the Allens, had some problems with their daughter. After the crisis, they gained some perspective about what would help them personally. Although they had always been community leaders, involved in many causes and attending many holiday parties, they chose the last week of December to literally go deep into the woods. They took a quiet camping trip and skipped all of the Christmas week hoopla. Although their pastor asked their relatives where they were, and some friends missed them at services and at parties, nothing major happened as a result of their decision. They made arrangements to see close relatives early in the new year, which was more relaxing and didn't include pressures like gifts and big meals.

Another couple changed their tradition of hosting a catered dinner for relatives and instead had a huge, informal get-together. They invited all of their friends and their family to come over for drinks and dessert. They bought some wine at a discount store, some prepared desserts, and some bake-it-yourself cookie dough. They cut up and served some fruit, and everyone just relaxed. They found it a nice change from all their usual preparations and expensive dinner courses.

As with a lot of things in life, the key to managing this situation seems to be preparation. Thinking ahead lets you be in control rather than overwhelmed when major holidays arrive. Because we are traditional Jews, there is no end to the cycle of holidays. Early autumn is especially full of holidays. My Scottish friend couldn't believe there was another one coming. Gary started making them up after a while ("No, really, it's Yom Chuchucha—we have to go make a fifty-thousand-calorie meal now").

Because holiday values and preferences are highly idiosyncratic, make your own personal list of the things you like best about each holiday. It might include things like sleeping late, special foods, rituals, or traditions, watching a favorite film—whatever speaks to you.

Then write down or discuss the things that *bother* you. List the holiday activities you dislike that you can get away with not doing this year. It's okay to do things differently; give yourself permission. Just because you've always hosted a Thanksgiving dinner doesn't mean you always have to. You can ask your brother and his wife to do it this year. Consider alternatives like a family picnic or a progressive dinner, in which several homes participate and guests eat a different course at each house.

If you can pinpoint which things make your holiday time a pleasure, you can better get in touch with how to proceed. Find out from your partner if there is openness to change. Nobody wants to bust up the family at Thanksgiving, but you may be surprised to find that everyone would be more than delighted to celebrate in a national park or at your sister's house for a change.

Find out approximately what the holiday will actually cost you. You may decide to invite your children or your grandchildren out to dinner instead of having a huge party at home. You can always go back to your original holiday plan next year.

Consider alternate ways of entertaining. Discuss your plans with your friends. One pair of friends found that they could share holiday food trays and other items from a warehouse club store, supplying two parties for less than the price of one.

Are Toxic People Ruining Your Holiday?

Do other people turn your good time into a bad one? In her book *Toxic People: 10 Ways of Dealing with People Who Make Your Life Miserable*, Dr. Lillian Glass points out that sometimes toxic people are toxic only for you. That is, their manner and comments offend only your sensibilities, not your friend's. It's a nice, nonjudgmental approach because it recognizes that human interactions are complex.

Give yourself permission to avoid people who add stress to your holidays. Wish them well, and let them be with people who don't experience them the way you do. We try so hard to make things work, but sometimes, particularly when things haven't been going well, using our emotional resources to make things work just isn't worth it. Enjoy the holiday, even if there are changes. Anything that relaxes you and your partner is a good option.

Barbara and Rick's Permission to Do Christmas Differently

Barbara and Rick are a couple in their late twenties who have experienced a disquieting summer and fall. Shortly after returning to work from a three-month maternity leave for the couple's first child, Barbara lost her job at the law firm where she had been an associate for three years. In spite of her Ivy League education, she couldn't make a transition to another firm. Rick had an administrative position at a small museum, and his hours and salary had been cut. They had very little desire to celebrate. They were feeling isolated and strange as the Christmas season approached.

Rick couldn't afford a nice gift. Barbara said that she understood, but he still felt "emasculated." When Barbara made a list of what she likes about Christmas, she showed Rick that expensive gifts truly weren't part of what made her holiday good. A gift was nice, but it was not all that important to the feeling of Christmas. Her list of holiday enjoyment included the following: time for the two of them to relax together while the baby was napping, looking at old photographs with her dad and hearing his stories, the smell of pine and evergreen in the house, Christmas cookies and eggnog, and friends laughing together. Barbara made sure Rick knew that they were a team and would get through this together.

Rick felt better seeing in writing the things that made Barbara enjoy Christmas and knowing that these things weren't out of reach. He made his own list, which enabled him to see how much he disliked all the holiday "had to's." They "had to" go to religious services with his family, they "had to" buy her parents an expensive gift, he "had to" attend the company's holiday party with her. Once they communicated their support for each other and really took a look at where their time and their money were going, they decided to do certain things differently. They made a "no gifts for the adults" declaration for this year (which made Barbara's recently retired parents happy) and bought iTunes gift cards for Rick's nephews. They found these at the grocery store while they were buying a few ingredients for cooking at home.

They decided that it wasn't necessary for Barbara to attend the company party. She didn't enjoy the rushed beauty appointments and leaving the baby with a sitter just to talk to office colleagues. Rick attended his company's party by himself, and he found that he was calmer and able to focus on his coworkers and his boss.

A couple who was good friends of theirs came to their house for a potluck dinner on Christmas Eve. This changed the family dynamic and allowed for lighter conversation that didn't include job problems. Barbara and Rick spent Christmas Day cooking a simple and delicious meal for other friends of theirs whom they knew to be in dire financial straits. It felt good for them to give. With the gift-giving and scheduling pressures gone, they were able to focus on the things that made them feel good together, and hosting their friends allowed them to give on a personal level.

Discussing the Holiday with Your Spouse

Diplomacy, diplomacy, diplomacy: turn "if I have to cook for days to hear your mother tell me one more time how nice it is for this generation to have so much help, I'll . . . " to "I'm not sure that all of the effort we put into the holiday meal for our family means much to anyone. We could prepare less, be more informal, and invite some other friends who'll make it more fun."

We're protective about our families, but we recognize that certain people can be difficult. Get back to focusing on your goal for the holiday and leave the old path behind, if necessary. If your goal is to spend meaningful time with your family, stressful preparations and formal dinners might not lead to this goal. Other ideas that still feed your guests but allow for much more fun and pleasant conversation might work. Be willing to try new things. Ask your spouse what his or her goal for this holiday is, write it down with yours, and then fill in the different ways the two of you can accomplish these goals.

Whether a Wall Street crash affects them or not, any family faces financial realities and disappointments. Couples need to make decisions about what's important to them and adjust their expectations, especially at a major holiday. They also need to be aware of their own expectations. It's sensible for a couple to agree not to exchange gifts this year, but when the day comes, will one of you be disappointed? Don't agree unless you're very sure you won't be let down in some way. It sounds good in theory, but in practice, abolishing gift-giving might diminish your happiness. Make sure the two of you are in agreement and that you create a holiday that both of you will enjoy.

Children and Holidays When Money Is Tight

When holiday discussions turn to children, many couples find themselves in emotional territory. One partner might feel guilty that there isn't enough money for exciting gifts. Parents might feel bad that they can't do what they did in the past to give their kids presents. Most children are aware that their family is having financial difficulties, being cautious for the future, and trying to rein in spending.

Josh and Lee's Story: **Antimaterialism or Rebellion against Mom and Dad?**

Josh, an attorney from the Upper West Side of New York, joined his best friend recently to open a small business. He and his wife, Lee, raise their two children as vegans. Josh, the son and grandson of wealthy entrepreneurs, is against the materialism that Christmas has come to represent, and he wants to raise their children without Christmas celebrations.

"Frankly, it's ridiculous," Lee points out. "It's like he's against whatever his parents did, so he wants to ruin Christmas for our kids. I like Christmas, and the children like toys and candy. They're going to see

211

other kids with toys, and they watch TV. I mean, we can't raise them in a bubble."

It's become a source of real contention in their relationship, because to Lee it indicates that Josh is willing to unconsciously put his own issues with his parents and his upbringing before the best interests of his children, notwithstanding that he cloaks it in anti-materialist rhetoric.

More than anything else in our lives, our children affect our good times and our bad times. We can dispassionately analyze our relationship with money, our need to control, and our hang-ups about our mothers, but we have seen rational people become completely unreasonable about an issue concerning their children. When the other parent of your child has a profoundly different viewpoint from yours, it's beyond upsetting, and when it involves finances, the emotions that are generated are often intense.

This reaction appears across the board. For straight couples and gay couples, Democrats and Republicans, people with a lot of money or with a small amount—when a couple disagrees about the children, it generates a lot of feeling. It may be tied to our belief that decisions that involve the children are endless in their possibilities. Maybe those piano lessons will allow Ryan to become the next Mozart or Ludacris.

"Look at the Williams girls," a couple thinks. "Their father got them into tennis, and, by God, if he could create successful kids through sheer force of will, we can, too." Some individuals become deeply resentful when their partners don't share their commitment, financial or otherwise, to a particular belief in the child. There's a lot of guilt at major holidays if you can't provide a "good holiday." For families experiencing serious hardships, these are times when guilt is better than going into debt.

Having a discussion about how money might have an impact on a holiday celebration goes a long way toward making everyone feel okay. The time to have this discussion with your kids is in October, well before the December holidays, not once the holiday has arrived. Saying something like "We can't do the things we did last year, and we need to discuss it. We want to enjoy our time together, and it would really help us if you could start thinking about the things you'd like now. There are three of you, and our budget is [fill in the number] dollars. Can you start thinking about things that would fall into that range? It would really help our family if we could plan this way."

Listen to your kids carefully, because helping children to focus on their goals (especially when presents are involved) as opposed to simply being locked on a path can make all the difference in the world. For example, suppose your son says he wants a certain game system. What he really might want is a *fun experience with* a game system, and perhaps that can be satisfied with last year's model. Maybe your daughter wants a certain MP3 player but would be satisfied with the one that holds two million songs instead of the one that holds more than the number of dollars in the U.S. debt. Through discussion you can get a feel for what your children are really wishing for and then possibly find a way to meet this request or help the children find a creative alternative. Certain clothing may make your kids feel cool and accepted, but maybe there is a different, less expensive item of clothing that could do the same thing.

Most children feel good about helping their family to enjoy holidays responsibly, and they feel good knowing that their parents are dealing directly with the realities. One caveat here, however: they also notice if the adults in their lives find money for their own needs and wants but make a minimum effort when it comes to spending on the kids. If there is money for Mom's expensive designer holiday clothes and the costly brand of Scotch that Dad gives his friends, but gifts for the kids have been pared down to nothing, that indicates a problem that is probably present year-round but that will be especially felt at holidays and remembered into adulthood. Examine the purchases for gift-giving holidays well ahead of time, set up a realistic and conservative budget, and then invite the family to be creative in other ways of celebrating.

Most children are aware of their family's situation in one way or another, and they appreciate thoughtful gestures like holiday crafts (you can find out about many creative ones through various Web sites and books) and special holiday food treats. They feel loved because their parents are making an effort to have as special a holiday as possible under the circumstances. This is your chance to teach your children some of the real meaning of most religious holidays: love of family, spirituality, and giving to others.

Most parents and children feel good about helping others. A series of different studies found that regardless of income level, people who spent money on others reported greater happiness than those who spent more on themselves. One study showed, according to its author, Elizabeth Dunn, that "even as little as five dollars may be enough to produce real gains in happiness on a given day."

No matter what the situation, most children can improve someone else's holiday. We visit the same nursing home on each holiday. The good feeling that your children will get from helping people, seeing them smile and enjoying your company, brightens any holiday. Many of the residents that we visit have

---

Enjoying Holidays with Less Money Than Before

1. Have an open discussion with your kids in October.
2. Discuss the fact that you're spending responsibly, what your approximate present budget is, and that you want to hear what they're expecting from the holiday.
3. Help them get a sense of what they want—the goal of what the present offers them instead of just the name of the present. Creatively try to satisfy the goal within your budget.
4. Children are often comfortable knowing that they're helping out the family by acting responsibly with their gift wishes.
5. Be aware of your own spending so that your children don't get the impression that there's money for others (family, coworkers, friends, yourselves) but not for them.
6. Show less guilt and more love and appreciation of their understanding.

outlived their families and friends. Often they want nothing more than to talk about politics, sports, or entertainment with someone. Some of the men in the residence we visit have invited the boys to play cards and board games.

We know that some people find nursing homes depressing or worry that their children will be frightened by residents who are not in full command of their faculties. We have never seen that reaction from even the smallest child, and we have taken along many kids from all sorts of backgrounds. A few teenagers who initially thought it was ridiculous to accompany their family later admitted that they enjoyed the visit. Other teenagers delivered gift packages and told their parents that it made them feel really good, even though they had initially thought it a "lame" idea.

Ten Gift Ideas for Kids

1. *For little children, get little presents.* Very small children are generally delighted with almost any age-appropriate little toy or interesting item that you give them. If the item is wrapped in pretty paper or has a balloon attached, the children will be delighted. There's no risk of an awkward moment in which the children report to their friends that they didn't get the really expensive doll or whatever. Parents often joke about how they bought expensive gifts for their toddlers and the kids were more interested in the boxes. Although we enjoyed big fancy gifts as children, the toys we played with endlessly were small green plastic soldiers and dolls with removable clothing. Spend less money on the little ones and apply the money saved to presents for the older ones.

2. *Ask parents who've been there and done that.* People who have kids older than yours may have ideas about which gifts, in retrospect, were a universal hit. Assuming that your kids don't have their hearts set on a specific thing, this is a good strategy for success. At one point we had five kids under the age of seven, with the eldest being six (yeah, we've heard the jokes) and we wanted to get something that would be fun for the group. A friend had kids who were a few years older, and she noticed that they loved the Fisher Price pirate ship. This was a well-received toy by our kids, an instant hit, and it was enjoyed for more than a decade. We later bought the Fisher Price castle; the princess joined the pirates on their ship, and it was all a lot of fun. Although some more classic toys like Lincoln Logs ended up being turned into weapons and lost, the castle and the pirate ship endured.

3. *Pool resources.* Relatives who would otherwise send cash will often enjoy the opportunity to participate in buying a more meaningful gift. You can let it be known that shares in little Johnny's new video game system are available—it might even be a nice way to honor your late uncle. You could affix a small plaque to the game unit reading something like "These joysticks are dedicated in loving memory to Lou Cohen." In fact, the honor of naming the entire playroom can be auctioned off to the highest bidding relative.

4. *Use the Internet.* Look on eBay and on overstock sites on the Web. Bartering sites offer chances to trade a marketable service for merchandise. Discounted merchandise is widely available.

5. *Have an old-fashioned sort of holiday.* Make decorations from instructions on craft Web sites, bake cookies, or dip pretzels or fruit in chocolate sauce. Giving kids special candy or fruits is a simple way to make the holiday festive. Make homemade gifts. Our neighbor made a tree house for his kids for Christmas using wood that his buddy had left over from a project. His kids took pictures of it and loved this gift more than any expensive gadget. What they valued was the time with Dad, the memory of working together as a team, and developing something from scratch. Whenever you make something with your kids, whether a tree house or cookies, the team effort and the time spent together tells your children that they are cherished.

   Amy Dacyczyn, in her classic *The Complete Tightwad Gazette*, talks about the lovely gifts she created through free, dime-store, and handmade materials. She recounts creating "doctor's kits" from sample items she got at doctors' offices and beauty bags for girls made with lip-gloss containers and nail polish in handmade little bags. When funds are painfully limited, gifts like these show thought for your children. They are obviously loving presents that cost no money but represent creativity and love.

6. *Take a trip.* Visiting a park or going camping by finding amazing rates on the Internet is a solid option for a holiday gift. Because we live in Florida, we often went to Disney World on holidays. We bought a one-day pass for each of our older kids (babies are admitted free), drove there and back on the same day, and had a memorable time. We brought along our own food and sodas. There are

often tourist attractions that can substitute for expensive material things, and time with family in a different setting is very memorable.

7. *Consider a pet.* If your financial situation and home life are reasonably stable and you have time and patience, a pet can be a sure way of generating excitement. Please be aware that bringing a pet into your home is a huge responsibility, not something to be undertaken impulsively. If you decide to get a pet, shelters are filled with puppies and kittens abandoned during foreclosures and other crises. The adoption fee is often nominal. The animal will have had all of the necessary shots, the implanted identity chip, and other veterinarian services that would cost at least a thousand dollars if you had to take care of them. Hamsters and their tunnel homes are inexpensive and very exciting for children, but be warned: hamsters do have a habit of disappearing from their cages and reappearing at inopportune moments.

8. *Give a group present.* Purchase something that the entire family can enjoy, like a Ping-Pong table or a new television. However, this option doesn't rule out little gifts for the kids. Warehouse and dollar stores can be good places to buy some inexpensive, individual toys to satisfy your children's wishes for some simple little gifts of their own.

9. *Observe the real meaning of the holiday.* Young couples with small children have a unique opportunity to establish simpler gift-giving traditions than the excess consumption that older kids have been conditioned to expect. Don't start out teaching your young children that a holiday is all

about fancy things; instead, focus on the actual meaning of the holiday. Institute this early, and your holiday seasons will always be about love and giving.

10. *Have fun!* No matter what gifts you give to your children, if there isn't a joyful spirit attached, you've wasted your money. We have the opportunity to give our kids fond memories of holidays that they can always draw on for a feeling of love and warmth. If a holiday is filled with stress and conflict, the gift isn't going to make it better. Make your holidays about fun and happy moments with your kids, and that will be the memory; a nice gift will just add background color.

12

Advice for the Worst of Times

Bad times, as we've said throughout this book, are a subjective concept. However, there is no denying that certain losses and the challenges that accompany them change us forever. When couples face tough times, they come away with a body of knowledge that others don't have—bought and paid for with the currency of heartbreak.

We spoke with four people for whom we have the utmost respect and who have managed to navigate truly bad times: the loss of a child, a terrible diagnosis, and the sudden death of a spouse and subsequent forging of a new relationship. Their personal observations of understanding, spirituality, and humor can aid and maybe even inspire us in dealing with our own bad times, for those were the qualities that got these people through the bad times, kept them together, and taught them important lessons.

Emily and Neil's Story: The Need to Find Meaning in Loss

Emily and her husband, Neil, are both children of Holocaust survivors. Emily, like many of the women she grew up with, speaks Yiddish and expected to live in the Orthodox Jewish community as a wife and a mother. Today she is a psychoanalyst, having completed a doctorate and postdoctorate work at the prestigious New York Psychoanalytic Institute. She runs a clinic that serves the mental health needs of the Brooklyn community. She is unusually accomplished academically, having been supported by her husband throughout her years of education.

She married Neil when she was twenty-one, expecting that they would live the life of an ultra-Orthodox Jewish family in Brooklyn. What changed this simple plan was their daughter, who at age two was diagnosed with a terminal illness. The medical treatments and the hospital stays were supplemented by home treatments, and Emily and Neil became proficient in the language of illness. Still in their early twenties, they had two other children, and they both worked to make ends meet. Neil worked from nine to five, so he was home to help the kids with their homework and make dinner while Emily attended graduate school. When their daughter died after several years of treatment, the hectic trips to the hospital and the intense decision making gave way to silence, and the couple had to learn to navigate their grief.

Their bad time lasted many years, and it didn't end with the death of their daughter. Emily and Neil found various ways to deal with their anger and sadness, but they never lost their generous kindness, sensitivity, and warmth. Emily will tell you that she and her husband coped in very different ways.

"How do I cope?" she asks rhetorically. "How do we cope as a couple? First of all, I really think we're troupers, that's for sure. It also helps that we've been together since we were twenty-one. We have decades behind us. What do we do to get through bad times? People cope differently; for me, talking helped and food helped. Neil operates differently from me. He has a macabre sense of humor, and I never appreciated that. But laughing and dark humor are what got him through. I have to say that spirituality and God helped us, too. A lot of people who suffer a trauma need to find meaning in it. I found that in religion. I personally found ritual soothing—the prayers.

"Both of us used music a lot. After our child's death, I needed music. We had a mourning period in which I didn't listen to music. Then as I drove to Brookdale every day for my doctorate, I turned on Barbra Streisand. I would start crying, and I found that very therapeutic; the music helped me to release the tears.

"You need a support system around you. Our friends and our family were there for us. Our friends took over our lives and were so supportive it was amazing. We went out inexpensively—we didn't try to control each other about money, we just kept going. But definitely our friends were amazing."

Because she is a therapist, Emily notices that whatever the situation may be, it helps a couple to find a way to be there for each other. "If you can find a rhythm with each other, then you'll know you are there for each other. You don't have to have the same individual rhythms. I don't take it personally when he goes into one of his moods. I just let it be, because I know that he handles his feelings differently from the way I handle mine. I'm a psychoanalyst, and his denial was hard to tolerate. Then I realized that he just needs to get through this his way. Some people need denial; it helps them get from here to there. Often there was dark humor for Neil.

"We were at a luncheon with an acquaintance of ours who knew that our daughter was very sick but probably didn't know that she had died. (Neil insists that the man was an idiot, that he had to have heard and forgotten.) The man smiled at us and loudly asked, 'So what's your daughter doing now?' Neil answered, with the same level of cheerfulness, "Oh, she's in real estate." Can you imagine? I had to sit there through the rest of the luncheon, unsure if I should set the record straight. I mean, what was I going to say at that point?

"I think that what a couple sees in its individual childhoods will obviously affect how it deals with difficulty. The families of origin, what the couple was like before the difficulties, how the mom and dad of each partner handled things—these are what adults in a crisis return to as a model.

"For me, a crucial thing is the ability of the spouse to soothe the other one. To show caring—for me it means holding me and saying, 'Don't worry, everything is going to be okay, and we're going to somehow get through this.' It's very individual. I need to be touched and soothed, to know that I can unburden myself and that the other person is going to be a good container for that. He's not going to fall apart, be judgmental, or try to have all the answers and solve all my problems. I want someone who can listen to me.

"A lot of us just want a 'good enough mother,' a psychological term for a mother who is just there. She contains the feelings you have. She's not perfect or all-giving, but someone who is just present with you.

"That's a big part of therapy, for many people: someone who can be there just to listen. A lot of people who suffer a trauma need to find meaning in it. That's why I turn to God."

For some people, talk therapy is a helpful option. Others benefit from the support of a group, either online or in person. Support groups are often found at local hospitals. There is usually no commitment of time or money, so trying it out is an easy option.

Melisa: Emily talks about the need for touch and the comfort it provides. I share this belief in touch as therapeutic. Gary and I experienced only a fraction of what Emily and Neil went through but when our baby Pacey was in the hospital, touch and massage seemed to dissipate some of the rage I was feeling at having "failed" as a mother by not having protected my child from this illness.

One of the doctors, sensing my feelings (was it the clenched teeth?) asked me if I thought I was a "magic mother" who could control the universe and prevent anything bad from ever happening to her child. Yes, I told him; actually, that is a mother's plan: to magically control the universe, to prevent all misfortune. He told me to try to relax, and I agreed that relaxing was a good idea, but I knew full well in my heart that all relaxation about my children's safety would probably elude me for the rest of my life.

The only time I wasn't churning with anxiety was during a massage. We all have the need to be touched, and it's often overlooked. For couples especially, friendly massage is wonderful. An article in *New Scientist* by Dr. Vilayanur Ramachandran of the Center for Brain and Cognition at the University of California, San Diego, notes that soldiers, including amputees, find that "massaging the skin helps relieve a painful sensation by restoring blood flow and activating sensory fibers that inhibit pain messages to the brain." It's not all in your head; touch actively changes brain chemistry and diminishes pain. Touch can be tremendously healing on many levels.

Giving ourselves permission to feel joy without worry is difficult. Worry creates a situation in which even good times have a shadow cast over them. Cognitive behavioral therapy techniques can be helpful in alleviating this worry. Visualizing the worst-case scenario and asking yourself, "How likely is this to happen?" puts things in perspective and can allow for more enjoyment of good times. Actively examining our premises and questioning them—not in a pressured, New Agey, positive-thinking-at-all-costs way, but in a quiet rewiring of our neurological worry pathways—can change how we are able to enjoy a situation.

Emily explained her challenges in good times. "For me, it's hard to enjoy the moment. I get nervous, I worry. Being a Holocaust survivor's child, I grew up with a lot of anxiety. Now, having been through a trauma, I am constantly waiting for the other shoe to drop. Neil does it, too. The other day we were up in the mountains visiting friends. I went for a walk, and Neil was waiting for me to get back. He was already worrying. 'What happened? You can get hurt, you could die, something could happen.' If things are going too well, you already wonder what's next."

Getting Through the Worst of Times

1. Tell yourself, "It's okay."
2. Get soothing words from loved ones.
3. Hear someone tell you, "It'll be okay."
4. Hear a loved one tell you that you are special.
5. Have a massage and other comforting touch.
6. Listen to music or sing out loud alone or with loved ones.
7. Recognize that your partner will deal with struggle differently, and don't take that personally.
8. Get some friend or neighbor community support.
9. Get some faith and religious community support.
10. Recognize that humor, often rather dark, is needed by some individuals to get them through tough times.
11. Trust in the passage of time; know that it will get easier in the future.
12. Allow your spouse to grieve in his or her own way.
13. Tell your spouse, "I'm grieving and am not able to meet your needs right now. Please don't take my need to be quiet right now as a rejection."
14. Revisit the methods of coping that have worked for you before.
15. Read aloud and to yourself.
16. Exercise (please do something you enjoy).
17. Go out in nature.
18. Consider medication.
19. Consider marital and individual therapy.
20. Sleep.

Religious connections and faith communities offer great support. Making music a part of your life and engaging in bonding activities like reading aloud and community service can also be very helpful. However, whereas some people, like Emily, seek meaning and comfort in faith, others don't, and while some find support in friends and in sharing their thoughts, others just need to be alone and quiet. Everyone has a different response to hard times.

Andrea's Story: Everyone Grieves Differently

Andrea takes her coffee black, her cigarettes full tar, and her realities unvarnished. She is in her early sixties and has been with her husband for forty-four years. She has lost many people in her life through death, including both parents at an early age and later her son. Andrea is not the kind of person who is given to self-pity or to placing much stock in current self-help theories. She runs her own business, doesn't do e-mail, and spends her time with her family and helping other people. If you compliment her on her good deeds and her philanthropic works, she will blow cigarette smoke at you and roll her eyes.

In response to Gary's questions about grief, she agreed that too often we forget that everyone is different and that each of us grieves differently. "If you don't require meaning," she said, "you accept the randomness of the universe and you move forward in your life, whether you want to or not. People try to reduce life to a recipe: If you do A, then B will happen, then C will occur, and then you achieve D. However, you're going to achieve D no matter what you do, in the sense that life moves on. We're forced to move forward by life itself."

"Why do you think a couple blames each other so much—during the bad times and especially, for instance, when there's a significant loss?" Gary asked.

"Well, it's much safer to blame each other," Andrea replied. "There are psychological issues at work here; you get mad at your spouse when you're really angry at your father. The all-powerful archetypal father, God, is scary to be mad at, so we don't get mad at God, we get angry at our partners instead. We blame our partners because it's easier, because it's better to blame them than to blame ourselves.

"The most important thing for both parties to do during any kind of stress is to recognize that there are going to be times in life when the other person can't meet your needs. People who are relatively self-aware know this. When you know that the other person is going through his or her own version of stress, you might have to take care of yourself at that time. When people think only about their own needs, that's when a couple breaks down. If children learn 'I am not getting all of my needs met right now, but I can meet my own needs for a while,' then later, in a relationship, they'll be much better able to navigate hard times. When they don't know how to do those things for themselves, problems arise. If you're in a situation with your partner and you know you're both struggling, you can manage by yourself for a while, knowing that your partner just can't meet your needs at that moment.

"Think about your grandparents," she continued. "I know you think of Grandma as the lady with the candy drawer, but you know, she and your other grandparents lived through a lot." Gary thought about them, picturing his sweet, calm grandmother. Grandma and her sister, Nana, had lost their brother to the 1918 flu pandemic. The sisters had married, lived through World War I and the Great Depression, raised their five children together in one three-generation house, and then sent four of their sons to fight World War II. All survived, with one of the boys landing on the beaches of Normandy as part of the D-Day invasion.

"It's true," Gary agreed.

"People of that generation had more realistic expectations," Andrea insisted. "They knew that there would sometimes be intense struggles in which their needs would not be met by their spouses. There are endless ways of coping. The passage of time in itself is important in dealing with trauma. Simply letting time go by seems to restore equilibrium. You have to understand that the other person is in as bad a shape as you are. Don't take it as a rejection that this person is coping differently from you. You know your partner. You know that going inward and not talking about the loss fits with his or her personality and the way that he or she does things."

If one partner in a couple has more of a withdrawing style than the other one does, then the introverted one should say something like this: "I need to get through this my own way. Let me be for a little while; I still love you." If people would articulate this, the anger and hurt of rejection could give way to understanding the real message: "This is how I handle this. I need some time; don't take it as a personal rejection."

For a couple to get through really bad times, the partners

need time itself as well as a real understanding that the other person is going through the same thing but is simply expressing it differently. If that awareness is there, then time itself will restore the balance.

Andrea noted that past generations seemed more patient. It is possible that people today are not used to exercising patience in having their needs met.

Donna's Story: The Glass Is Always Half Full

Donna is the most relentlessly positive person we know. She is endlessly upbeat. Years ago, when we were newly married, Donna met Melisa for lunch and told her that she had been diagnosed with a serious illness. Melisa was very upset, but Donna didn't seem to be particularly so. She was matter-of-fact; she told Melisa that she and her husband would take it day by day. Later, when it turned out to be a misdiagnosis, she was grateful and happy.

When Donna had trouble becoming pregnant, she didn't worry. She just consulted many different fertility specialists until she found the one who helped her become pregnant. Most of us would have been extremely stressed, but this woman just went on—and not in a forced, creepy way. It was amazing. When she finally did get pregnant, one of her twins disappeared from the sonogram; however, Donna just focused on the fact that one remained. Melisa always wondered how Donna stayed so positive. She didn't seem to take things to heart; she genuinely looks at the bright side and was thinking the best even as the doctor was looking upset.

"Well, the alternative—being depressed and angry—doesn't excite me," Donna explained. "I make a conscious choice to just say, 'It's okay.' If you don't say it's okay, you'll give in to making yourself crazy. I don't like negative feelings. I have them, and I know I'm going to have them, but I actively talk myself out of them. I say, 'Donna, you don't have to feel this way. You can wait and let it pass and then give yourself another message.'" Donna was actually describing a technique that is used effectively in cognitive therapy to change thought processes and their underlying premises.

Donna doesn't contain her feelings; she deals with them personally and in relationships. "I believe in talking to people if I'm upset with them. You have to let it out. I say to people, 'When this happened, it made me upset.' Without attacking them, I make it a point to tell them how I feel. I don't like conflict; I want to work it out. I deal with things to keep the dynamic positive. It's worth it to me. I stay away from negative people; I feel bad about it when I do, though. I also want to save people—such as people who are sad—and you do feel better when you give to people, so I try to give other people happiness. If I'm feeling crappy, I'll be in a bad mood, but if I get involved in giving, that changes my mood."

Working through feelings, changing the messages we give ourselves, actively saying it's okay, and giving to others are all techniques that are undeniably helpful in feeling positive. There are two more techniques that Donna disclosed, but they are not always available to everyone. "I have a friend in my spouse," she said. "My husband is my best friend, and I can depend on him. He'll listen to me vent, and he'll always be there for me." This was interesting, because some people believe that they have found their soul mate, and that makes a huge difference in how they cope during bad times.

Dolly Parton gave an interview in which she discussed her marriage of nearly forty-three years. She reported being happy with the little Valentine's Day chocolate box that her husband, Carl, brought her from the drugstore each year. She recalled that when she first met Carl, "The instant I saw him, it was just one of those things like a flash—I just knew him. I just knew. And the same with him. He knew. The spark was instant for both of us."

Obviously, Dolly's relationship has the positive communication we all need to build a deep friendship and meet each other's needs.

Donna not only has her husband, there is another important key to her positive state. "I have my mother," she explained. "I can talk to her about things, and she listens. My mother always made me feel good about myself. You need one person who says to you, 'You're wonderful.' It has to be from someone you respect as a child—a grounded source, someone who sees your flaws and really believes that you are capable. When you have a mother or another person like that, later on everything in life is easier. If you didn't have a person like that, it's important to be aware, when going through bad times, that you don't have that positive force in your life. Try to provide the voice that tells you how good you are and that you can get through this."

Alan's Story: Look for People Who Think You're Special and Are Happy to Say It

Alan lost his wife, Sandy, after a brief illness and was left to raise their daughter alone. There wasn't much money, but he worked hard and tried to be creative in pursuing success. He built a business and put his daughter through college. Through it all, he tried to stay positive. He admitted that it wasn't easy, and he spent many lonely nights wondering why this had happened to his family. He relied on his brother and his friends and tried to create a new life. Exercise and trying to establish routines helped him.

"I laugh at situations, I laugh at myself, and I work out," said Alan. "All that helped, but if I had to pinpoint the things that helped me after Sandy's death, I'd have to honestly say that it was drugs and talk therapy. It's not a popular answer, I know, but therapy and drugs were very, very helpful to me. They allowed me some distance from it all, and they let me do what I needed to do. I probably could have 'gotten through' it without the prescription, but would I have been able to raise my child well and work? I don't know. Would I have been able to date and find a wonderful relationship? I don't think so."

Alan isn't a desperate type. He's calm and measured, well spoken, and very impressive. That may be why he was able to separate himself from the stereotypes and old misconceptions about "needing drugs" or "needing to see someone" and do what he needed to cope. "I find it interesting that people will just absolutely not consider medication because they see it as a character failing or as using a crutch, but they'll suffer needlessly and not be okay. I see people every day who are obviously depressed or having a hard time. They're ashamed to get some help; instead, they think it's better to explode or turn to alcohol or recreational drugs. I really don't get that. I mean, I like a beer or a drink as much as anyone else does, but I do know people who will just drink and drink to numb the pain and look at you as if you're crazy when you suggest Prozac. Some people think that you're a failure or something if you need to treat depression, but depression sometimes requires treatment. One lady started talking to me about the herb St. John's wort [which is said to help depression]; that was fine for her, but it didn't do it for me."

Alan went to a group therapy meeting for bereaved spouses, but he found that he didn't like sharing in such a public way. He asked his daughter's pediatrician to recommend a therapist for his daughter, and he found his own therapist through that referral as well. Today his daughter is grown, and he looks back on that time as the worst time of their lives. Coming out of it, finding love again, and working in a business of Alan's own were all made possible by the help he was willing to get.

Notes from the Field: What Gets You Through

Here are some methods for getting through difficult periods that have been suggested by others who've been in the worst of times but have remained positive and resilient.

Spirituality

Spirituality is really important—not only a belief in God, but the idea that there is a larger universe with which to connect. From the time we are born until we finally approach death, our lives are made up of small moments of intense beauty and connections. Identifying those moments can help you transition from panic or fear to a better feeling. It seems to get people through the bad times by giving them perspective.

Although there is desperation, overwhelming loss, or fear in one's life, gratitude, love, and beauty can provide some momentary healing. For those who are comfortable with the idea of having a relationship with God, make this relationship an active one in which you see yourself as both a partner and a child of the godliness. You never are alone. Talk to God not only with prayers of need but also as simply a means of sharing and connecting with an eternal source of goodness and strength. Rely on this strength and feel your godly connection grow within your spirit.

Music

Melisa: Everyone I have spoken to listens to music. Music allowed Emily the cathartic release of her emotions as she drove to school. It gave her husband's rage a vicarious voice. He played loud classical music, with cymbals crashing. He played heavy metal music as he diapered their children. Music accesses interesting neurological areas in our brains. It is unquestionably a source of comfort and release in good times and in bad.

When my own parents had a child with Down syndrome in 1975, my sister and I were genuinely concerned about the survival of our family. We were nine and seven, respectively, and although

236

our classmates were kind, other kids on the bus and in school called us names and imitated what they imagined our sister would be like. At that time, many special-needs children were institutionalized, and it wasn't common to see people who were different in that way. One religious teacher informed us that it was "God's way of punishing parents for something they'd done." Nice. I spat my gum into her purse when she wasn't looking.

Although it might be unrealistic to suggest that we can simply get through hard times as a couple through music, it is possible to use music to create a small moment, and that moment can help us to find other ways to draw close in our relationship. Singing songs as a family almost always produces a sense of spirituality, love, and togetherness.

The most interesting thing about music (and laughter) is that it costs nothing, or almost nothing. The radio, family singing, and church and synagogue choirs are readily available. Kids find older-model iPods on the Internet today for surprisingly low prices. Take a moment to analyze how much music is in your life personally and as a family. Can you join others for singing or attending a concert? Some people start their day with music, listening to something uplifting.

As a child, I learned that music very comforting, and singing in the school choir was a positive way of coping. The songs my friends and I learned in the choir, both traditional religious songs and popular songs, are ones we still sing together from time to time. Some of us have even taught them to our kids. I had an unusually connected class growing up, and those friendships have endured for more than thirty years. I wonder if singing together creates a bond that makes closeness easier to achieve. Music certainly does good things for you, as an individual and as a couple.

Revisit the Methods That Have Worked Before

Because each of us finds different things helpful, it's worthwhile to think about your personal history. Recall your childhood, your teens, and early adulthood. What gave you help in the past? What, if anything, helped foster connections to the people in your life or allowed you to manage on your own?

One man remembered the welcome outlet that sports afforded him when he was growing up with an explosive father. He joined a community basketball league and found it very helpful in dealing with his current work problem.

Miriam, a woman in her fifties, remembered starting at a new school in junior high and being excluded from every clique and social group. She recalled that getting a job after school had provided her with another place to go, in both a physical and an emotional sense. She realized that in her adult life, relocating to a new city for her husband's work had given her a similar feeling of loss and of not really belonging. She began volunteering at a local women's shelter, taking pleasure in having an outlet and a place to go.

Read Aloud

Melisa: When I went to school in the 1970s, we sat in little groups on a carpet and did our assignments. It was nice to structure our work time the way we wanted and to have interesting discussions with other students. Nobody yelled at us for talking to our neighbors—in fact, we were encouraged to work together on our individualized math packets.

Because all of us scored well on the regular achievement test in those days (though nobody's funding depended on it), our teacher could "waste time" reading aloud while we relaxed on the reading rug. Many teachers would say there isn't time in today's classroom for the hours of reading aloud that we enjoyed. That's a shame, because the result of those hours was a group of kids who became lifelong readers—who felt the primitive, comforting feeling that most of us associated with books. In *The Read-Aloud Handbook*, Jim Trelease extols the numerous benefits of reading aloud: an improved cognitive ability, an advanced vocabulary, a mysteriously enhanced ability to extrapolate from one idea to another, and an inherent appreciation for sentence structure and the use of language.

What I have observed and return to, however, is the shared sense of belonging you feel as you hear a story being read aloud. It must be encoded in our DNA from early tribal gatherings around the campfire. This is the bonding event my own children remember with the most enthusiasm. Of all the techniques we employ, we have relied on nothing as much as reading aloud to keep us connected in difficult times. In good times and bad, consider reading aloud regularly as a family. Listening to audiotapes is also a good shared activity for adults.

Not every good book lends itself to being read aloud. Here are some we have particularly enjoyed, in ascending age-appropriate order. I have noticed that younger kids (in the absence of television or video games) often enjoy listening to books read to their older siblings.

Classics like *Goodnight Moon*, *The Very Hungry Caterpillar*, *Brown Bear*, the Little Bear series, *Where the Wild Things Are*, the Dr. Seuss books, Bible stories for children, and Disney fairy tales provide outlets for children's complex feelings. (For more on that, read *The Uses of Enchantment* by Bruno Bettelheim.)

There are thousands of books for small children. Read what you and they enjoy. Here are some suggestions:

The Young Biography series: short books on famous people

Tuck Everlasting by Natalie Babbitt

The Little House series and *Farmer Boy* by Laura Ingalls Wilder (Some kids do find parts of these books boring, so we skipped around.)

All-of-a-Kind Family by Sydney Taylor (Some boys won't like it.)

The Harry Potter series by J. K. Rowling

The Pendragon series by D. J. McHale

From the Mixed-Up Files of Mrs. Basil E. Frankweiler by E. L. Konigsburg

For older kids, the books that will make them laugh and cry include the following:

To Kill a Mockingbird (twelve and up) by Harper Lee. If you read it in school and only vaguely remember it, please take another look. It's an amazing story and a fabulous read-aloud.

The Navigator by Eoin McNamee

The Secret Life of Bees by Sue Monk Kid

The Adventures of Huckleberry Finn by Mark Twain. Ernest Hemingway once said that all American novels derive from this one. This fantastic story always sparks discussion, especially about social mores and individual responsibility.

Exercise

Melisa: I'm not a big fan of exercise. My family members didn't flee the Russian czar and cross the ocean so that their descendants could one day run mindlessly on a machine to nowhere. I really try, but I have a bad attitude, and while my husband and my sons run marathons, I stand on the sidelines and smile and wave, then stagger off gratefully to my bed, truly not understanding it. Why are they running twenty-six miles? Is it a jail sentence? Did they offend someone?

Still, the data are in, and the news isn't good for people like me, who would rather watch *House* or old *Seinfeld* episodes than do aerobics and lift heavy things.

Exercise is key; it really is. It works as well as an antidepressant in many studies. It's the fountain of youth. When you exercise, the chemical changes are real. You boost serotonin, the feel-good brain chemical; you create endorphins; and you stave off a whole host of diseases. There's a better chance you'll weather the bad times if you're moving.

The simplest exercise is walking. Walking together as a couple is nice. You can talk about ideas, foster creativity, and connect. If you're walking alone, you can listen to music, if you have one of the myriad modern listening devices (which you'll probably have to have one of your kids show you how to use).

Taking a walk to somewhere is a good date, even if it's going for coffee or to a friend's house. Yoga classes are given on television, community centers offer tennis, and there are many other options. People who are active seem to find something they enjoy doing and then create time in their day for doing it. When exercise time becomes inviolate to someone, you know that this person makes his or her health a priority. If you can combine exercise with a social activity, the health benefits increase. Exercise ranks high in strategies for coping.

Medication

Different medications might be indicated to help you through your struggle. Medication does not mean that you won't be doing any personal work to heal or manage the crisis, but it can take the edge off and lighten your load during bad times. Some people feel very uneasy about the whole meds thing, which we understand. There are side effects to medication, including suicide risks, in some rare cases.

Nevertheless, when people are seriously depressed, unable to move and function properly, or having suicidal thoughts, they shouldn't avoid medication because they think society will look down on them. In addition to antidepressants, which have to be taken regularly for a period and don't take full effect for a couple of weeks, there are antianxiety medications that can be taken as needed with immediate effect, to soften some moments of extreme anxiety or desperation. Consult with a psychiatrist instead of your general doctor to find out whether these medications are for you and also to have someone to be in touch with while you're on these drugs.

Therapy

Look into getting help from others, whether in couples therapy or short-term cognitive behavioral therapy. Some people benefit from longer therapy; it really is just another tool for dealing with what life throws at us. Be clear about your goal and make a general plan with the therapist that includes an estimate of how long the therapist thinks you'll need to accomplish your goals.

There are many other forms of therapy besides the classic ones. Talking to someone older than you who has a soothing influence as well as some creative ideas is helpful for most people. Find a mentor or rely on a wise and caring sibling or best friend. Seek out the support of clergy and others who can give you a sense of comfort and belonging.

Sleep

Melisa: Carla worked hard at looking good. Her hair was straightened, she worked out regularly and was nicely dressed. But if you looked at her eyes, they were bleary and she was jittery from too much espresso.

Carla and Conrad's son, Joel, who was about to turn twelve, was diagnosed with autism, which qualified him for a special school. Joel chewed through all their telephone cords and computer equipment wires. The plumber should just have been given a key to the house, because Joel was constantly throwing items into the toilet.

Carla found that music and working out helped her cope. She also tried to attend religious services, which she she enjoyed, and she had a network of friends and a good support system. Recently, though, Conrad had had to change careers because of the economy. A side effect of all the changes was that her husband, when he wasn't tossing and turning, snored at what she swore were explosion-level decibels.

Carla looked distracted. She probably was; a chronic lack of sleep can send you over the edge.

"You know, don't you, that they torture prisoners of war this way?" I asked.

"It works," she replied. "I'll tell you anything you want." The sleep deprivation caused her to drive weirdly, so I tried not to ride with her very often.

Unfortunately, Carla was insistent on driving us to lunch that day at a little place we like near the popular boardwalk. She narrowly missed hitting a scantily clad six-foot woman in stiletto-heeled boots. "What was that outfit?" she asked.

"I don't know. I was too busy hoping you weren't going to actually kill her."

"Oh, she was fine. You know, if I could just sleep, I would feel so much better. I don't even remember what it was like to feel rested. I get no uninterrupted sleep. Part of the problem is the financial thing. Conrad is worrying, and he wants to discuss it all at midnight. Then, sometime after three, maybe I'll really start sleeping. Joel comes into our room every morning at six. All of that I could maybe deal with, but the biggest thing is the snoring. It is *un-be-liev-a-ble*." As she parked, the car hit the curb and jumped onto the sidewalk.

"Damn. Was that sidewalk always there?"

"Yeah. Since the eighties. Wow, driving with you is special."

"You're special," she muttered.

"I don't understand this, Carla. I care about you, and it doesn't make sense to live like this. You have a special-needs child who chews the cords on your electrical appliances, you have two other kids, and you can't function because you don't sleep. You're smart. What is this?"

"In college once, I didn't sleep for like three nights during finals, and on the drive home I saw clowns. When I start hallucinating clowns, I'll deal with it."

The paradox of sleep deprivation is that once we're sleep-deprived, we can't make good decisions, and then we just become more sleep-deprived, leading to more disoriented decision making. Getting good sleep is an important key to keeping ourselves going in bad times. When we have enough sleep, we are less impatient with our partners, our children, our coworkers, and the guy at the service counter. When we're overtired, we can't even communicate well, let alone deal with problems creatively.

In Carla's case, her husband's snoring was the thing she couldn't manage. It's a good idea to rule out sleep apnea or other medical problems that can cause very loud snoring, but Conrad was unwilling to be checked out. Antisnoring devices didn't help, so she finally decided to sleep in her daughter's spare bed for a few nights each week. This allowed her to get herself back together until she could figure out other options.

Carla strongly believed that curtailing Joel's time in their bed would be a deprivation for him, so she began going to bed earlier, turning off the television, darkening the room, and taking a hot bath an hour before bed. She read a magazine instead of watching a medical drama. All these cues gave her body the message to fall asleep earlier. She told Conrad that worrying about finances wasn't going to solve anything, and they agreed not to discuss problems after dinner.

They stopped drinking after dinner, too, because alcohol may put you to sleep, but once it's metabolized it interferes with sleep, leading to middle-of-the-night wake-ups. Conrad

~~~~~~

Sleep Information

It's estimated that 20 percent of Americans sleep fewer than six hours a night, up from 13 percent eight years ago. Sleep is a $23.9 billion industry; it's gone up 50 percent in the last decade, according to a study cited in the *New York Times.* The market for insomnia drugs alone is expected to grow 78 percent annually, to nearly $3.9 billion, by 2012.

An alternative to popular drugs is a program called cognitive behavioral therapy (CBT) for insomnia. It changes the way people's thoughts and habits prevent good sleep. A study published in the *Journal of the American Medical Association* found that "patients who used both therapy and zolpidem (the generic name for Ambien, the prescription sleep aid) fared better during the first six weeks of the study. But by the six-month mark, subjects who relied on behavioral therapy alone made the most progress."

Proponents of CBT say the results are wonderful, but people with conditions like severe anxiety or bipolar disorder should probably discuss the program with their doctor.

There is an online version of CBT for insomnia available for twenty-five dollars at www.cbtforinsomnia.com. A study found that 95 of 118 subjects (81 percent) who used online behavior therapy reported improved sleep.

More sleep suggestions can be found at the Web site of the American Academy of Sleep Medicine (http://www.sleepeducation.com).

~~~~~~

discussed a prescription sleep aid with his doctor, but he used it for only a few nights. Although the challenges of dealing with a special-needs child remain formidable, both Carla and Conrad recognize that starting the day exhausted is not a good option. By implementing these changes, they have allowed themselves to approach their challenges a little better.

They began to be nicer to each other, and that led to sharing more feelings. Carla and Conrad began to realize that closeness that had been lacking between them. She was less resentful of him as a result of her better sleep, and he felt better able to share his concerns.

If your bedroom isn't a pleasant place, consider what would work better for you. It could be the bed itself: Is it restful? Although there isn't any real proof that a special mattress helps people to sleep, sleeping on a mattress that is uncomfortable certainly doesn't help.

Sleep experts and people who study insomnia point out that we sleep best in a temperature of around seventy-five degrees. Are the textures surrounding you comfortable? Is the pillow the one your husband used in college? Are the sheets uncomfortable? High-thread-count cotton sheets can be found at various discount stores. Create order and calm in the bedroom; it can pay off in a good night's sleep.

If your partner likes having heated discussions at night, agree to a prearranged signal that both of you know means "Stop. This isn't going to end well, and we cannot discuss this until tomorrow." It might be a phrase like "Not tonight. We need to sleep," or some meaningless phrase that stops the fireworks before they start. This technique may seem silly, but it works for a lot of people. A word or a short phrase that stands for a prearranged set of rules and understanding can be used at times like that to preserve the peace.

Nature

A recent study found that being in a natural setting is good for your brain. The researchers gave the subjects a short memory test and then took them to a park, where they walked around for an hour. They were then given a similar test, and it was found that they performed on average 20 percent better. The time spent in nature improved their cognitive ability. The results were similar for subjects who spent an hour viewing nature scenes on a screen. A control group that walked around the city showed no improvement.

It appears that being in nature boosts cognitive ability by providing the brain with a setting in which we are engaged but the brain can rest.

Thoreau was right. Go to the woods. Plan a picnic, hike or walk the trails. Find a park near you.

Humor

Humor can save your sanity at difficult times. It's not a replacement for any of the coping techniques we've outlined but serves as an important supplement. Find funny television shows, movies, books, and people to make you laugh. The people we interviewed for this chapter availed themselves of the release that laughter can provide. Humor can take many forms, but whatever the form, allow humor to be part of your coping.

Epilogue

Gary has never been one to say, "Hey, you think you have it bad? Look at so-and-so; now *that's* bad." When you hear that, you figure that the person who said it doesn't really want to hear you out or has judged you as some kind of whiner. Yet at times in our lives, especially with financial concerns, it helps to put your life in perspective.

After our son Pacey lived through his illness, we quickly learned about real struggle. For an extended period, it made Gary even more of a nervous Jewish guy, who took to responding to the question "How are the kids doing?" with a short "They're still alive." After the dust had settled a bit, we knew that ultimately we had been blessed, and we had to force ourselves to start learning from this tough period.

One simple lesson was what to worry about and, more important, what *not* to worry about. To this day, fourteen years later, when one of us is becoming a little too stressed about something that is not health-related, the other one will pull out our calming signal and say, "Hey, who's sleeping at the hospital tonight?" This refers to the thirty-five nights we had to decide who was sleeping with our sick child at the hospital and who was staying home with his twin and his three siblings, ages one, four, and six.

Our use of this signal is never meant to diminish the right to be worried or stressed, but simply to diminish the *intensity* of it. It's done with love and often a hug or a quick kiss so that it's never confused with an "I don't care to listen" message. It's always followed up with a commitment to listen and be a sounding board for the one who is stressed. It settles us down a bit and helps us put it all in perspective.

Things get better, and when they do, you'll have the wisdom to stop and appreciate that good time. It's something we all struggle to do: maintain perspective, find love together, and turn toward each other to get through the bad times and fully celebrate the good.

Vow Renewals

If you've turned your relationship around and now feel more like a team, consider renewing your vows. This renewal can represent a new stage of your marriage, showing that you have come through a trying situation and have learned to be united through it all. When people first take their wedding vows, they wax poetic. It sounds lovely, especially with the musical accompaniment and people tearing up. Quite often, however, we make these vows without a great deal of understanding of their true meaning. Once you've been through an experience that tests your vows and you both feel an increased closeness and a strengthened marriage from the trying time, renewing your vows can be very meaningful.

This time around, you'll be making vows to each other that have tremendous meaning and understanding behind them. You'll be recognizing what your marriage is really about. Taking the time to mark the next level of your life partnership is very worthwhile. The ceremony can take on any form that works for you, whether religious, with family and friends, or even just the two of you. Spend time independently to consider what you've been through and how you've worked together to grow as a couple. Write vows that reflect what the other person has meant to you through this time, and compose some promises for the future.

You don't have to be over your struggle in order to do this. You are just clarifying for yourself and your spouse how crucial your relationship has been to maintaining an emotionally healthy and balanced life through thick and thin.

Be specific. Timothy, the husband who appeared on *Oprah*, added as part of his vows that he would consult a physician in the future the moment his wife suggested it. Since she was scared that he would one day fall back into a depression and return to an unmovable state of sadness, he had to reassure her that he'd seek help long before it became as intense as it had been before. Even if he didn't think he needed to go for help, as long as Amy requested it, he'd do it. Amy vowed to fight for her marriage, and that sent a powerful message, now that she understood how much she was willing for fight for their lives together.

The vow renewal is a moment to have a mental high-five and confirm what the two of you have learned and will continue to build on in the future.

In times of struggle, remind yourselves that things really can change significantly and quickly. If you knew today that things would be much better one year from now, you'd feel immediately relieved.

Envision that. Take a moment now and later to close your eyes and see past this time to the way you want your situation resolved. Believe in yourself and in the people and the love around you.

Index